ECHOES BEYOND

Written by Patsy Greenway

Co-Authored by Christine Saunders

Illustration by Jason Greenway

Author: Patsy Greenway

Contributing Co-Author: Easter Christine Saunders

Published in the United States by: Patsy Greenway

Line Editor: Fiona Claire

Formatting by: Tammy Compton Mckee

Cover Design by: Anita B. Carroll   www.race-point.com

ISBN-13:978-1505579543

ISBN-10:1505579546

Based on a true story, names of some people and some places have been changed.
This book is written in memory of our mother, Clara Bell Arnold Compton, and
dedicated to Cole, Jess, Samuel and Bethany Saunders.

Clara Bell Arnold

PART 1: BLACK TOP MOUNTAIN

CHAPTER ONE

Accordin' To Momma

The unwelcome sunlight forced its way through the leaves adorning the high tree tops, in spite of the thick black dust blanketing each one. It unmercifully ushered in another day of awful dread to those living on Back Top Mountain. My daddy found himself among those unfortunate souls struggling against widespread poverty with few opportunities to find a way to survive the mountain's cruelty. Daddy rendered some hard blows to the mountain hiding black coal deep within its steep ridges, but he could not escape its sway. That is, until he met a teenager named Clara Arnold. As a result, his life and the world around him would be changed forever. The cruelty of the massive heap cowered at her unwavering tenacity to survive its vengeance and her daring attempt to raise twelve children beneath its tall timbers.

My daddy, Luther Patton Compton, the fourth child born to Whitten Compton and Gertrude Brown, came into the world on February 7, 1911. Grandma and Grandpa had a prearranged marriage by Grandma's daddy. At the time of the marriage, Grandpa had passed his thirty-second birthday and Grandma only her sixteenth. Being part of a large family with five brothers and five sisters made life especially difficult for Daddy while growing up on Black Top Mountain. The mountain had rightly been named, being a place of darkness and despair offering no easy way out for those born on its unforgiving perch.

Daddy attended school very little, choosing to help care for his siblings instead. Empty milk buckets and crying babies accentuated the need.

Grandpa, on the other hand, spent much time reading the many books lining a bookshelf in his bedroom, along with the Bible. His hellfire and brimstone preaching attracted the worst of sinners.

According to Momma, in 1929 a young lady named Lila Jones cast her flashing blue eyes on my Daddy. Soon wed by the Justice of the Peace, they moved into a cozy log cabin on Black Top Mountain. Grandpa, along with family members, built the cabin on land his father acquired shortly after the Civil War through the Homestead Act. The Homestead Act required the land to be farmed for five years and then the "homesteader" became the owner.

The Great Depression began the same year. However, life had always been more than challenging for those on the mountain, with long winters and few crops in the summer, so the Great Depression found no place to settle on Black Top

Mountain. Poverty had already laid claim to the territory.

A few months into the marriage Lila realized she was pregnant. When the baby boy arrived he lived only a few hours. Almost a year later, Lila gave birth to another son, naming him Spencer Lee.

What the mountain folks called "moon shining" became Daddy's choice of employment to make ends meet. Shinin' had its advantages seeing as how his Uncle, Tom Compton, held the office of local sheriff and became a regular customer. Momma said it wasn't unusual to hear the uncle chide Daddy about "gettin' caught by the law one of these days" with loud laughter following the remark. The mountain folks still consider this to be a *"real knee slapper!"*

Despite hard times, Daddy had many regular customers join him in the damp cellar dug out beneath the cabin. The cellar, intended to house fresh produce and canned goods, soon had Mason jars filled with illegal moonshine lining its shelves.

As with any entrepreneur, backwoods or not, Daddy spent more time with customers and less with his family. The profession he choose didn't offer Lila the fine clothes and fancy hairdos she daydreamed about. She saw pictures in the magazines in the *"johnny house"* outback. The women modeled ruffled dresses and wore face paint. Their curled hair lacked the need to beg for attention. Not having any of these luxuries, she soon tired of Daddy's drinking and her daydreaming.

Lila tried, to no avail, to persuade her husband to get a "real" job. Daddy paid her no mind, and that decision he later regretted.

On the bitter cold morning of the 26th day of December in 1936, my daddy's youngest brothers, Collin, aged nine, and Ralph, aged twelve, awoke to the sound of unfamiliar voices. While the cold wind howled outside, they quickly dressed in bib overalls with threadbare flannel shirts underneath and slid their bare feet into cracked leather boots with turned up toes. Making their way down the creaky wooden stairs, they noticed neighbors crowding into a small room next to the kitchen.

Collin and Ralph walked slowly to the corner of that small room where their mother lay motionless on a bare mattress held up off the floor by rusty railings attached to an iron frame. The soft glow of a nearby oil lamp revealed the dispassion of death. Daddy, standing nearby, embraced his youngest brother, Collin, as irrepressible sobs penetrated the air. Ralph turned and ran outside to escape the chill of death.

This seemed a lot for two young children to endure, especially when Christmas day arrived with nothing to look forward to.

The next day kind neighbors made sure the cold hard mountain soil received the homemade pine box containing the lifeless body of Gertrude Compton, only forty eight years old. She had waged war against Black Top Mountain and lost. A small headstone, leaving a compendious imprint on the cold mountainside, became a witness to all who visited the large graveyard. Surrounded by rotting fence rails with tall brown entangled weeds clinging to the fence posts, the graveyard seemed to be forgotten much like those laid to rest inside its boundaries. All who gathered to say good-bye knew many more would lose their struggle against the fierce anger of an invaded mountain and be swallowed up by its hatred for life.

According to Momma, Daddy didn't allow the loss of his mother to interfere with his shinin' business. Another reminder of just how bad life could be on the mountain seemed all the more reason for the locals to drink.

As Daddy's time with customers increased even more, he and Lila began to argue almost daily. Then the arguments with Daddy escalated. With little concern for Lila's feelings, he continued making and selling moonshine.

Sometimes the customers stayed awhile to visit. If weather permitted, they sat on the front porch. The more moon shine they drank, the better it tasted.

One warm breezy afternoon Daddy, along with moonshinin' customers, enjoyed the luxury of the front porch. The contents of a Mason jar dwindled while the men conversed as usual. The dominant mountain tops echoed the sound of laughter.

The wooden ladder back chair Daddy occupied made a thud, the result of the two front legs coming to an abrupt stop on the porch floor. Previously, the chair rested against the post directly behind it. Daddy often leaned the chair backwards, the mark on the post bearing witness to that. However, the squeak of the rusty hinges attaching an old wooden door to the cabin, startled him and he quickly leaned forward.

Lila's feminine frame stole the attention of the male visitors. The plangent chirping of a nearby robin proclaimed winter's end. A cloud of smoke from lit cigarettes and a stench from cheap moonshine fouled the fresh mountain air.

"Patton, I need some groceries from the store," Lila informed her husband matter-of-factly.

"I'll go dreckly," Daddy assured her.

Lila spun around to go back in the cabin. Glancing up, her eyes met with those of one of the men sitting on the other side of the porch. The magnetic attraction denied her the energy to take another step. She watched his eyes wander down her small stature and stop at her full bosom.

The sound of Daddy's voice made Lila jump. "Are you alright, Lila?"

"Yes—yess—ah fine" Lila faltered, quickly stepping back into the cabin and closing the door behind her. She leaned her back against the closed door, both hands clinging to the door knob. Her blushing face and weak knees reminded her of a foolish school girl. With heart racing, she couldn't recall my daddy ever eyeing her like that.

Lila peeled potatoes and tried to focus on her commitment to Daddy, but her mind kept wandering back to the man on the porch and how she longed for a better life away from the mountain.

The scuffling sound on the front porch announced the men's departure. Lila glanced out the curtain less window and saw Daddy leaving, too.

Lila put Spencer down for his nap, then walked over to a nearby ladder-back chair with a railing missing underneath, and sat down. The chair wobbled in resistance to her weight, threatening to give way beneath her, but it held together. She pondered whether or not she and Daddy would have another argument when he returned home. Lost in her thoughts, the sudden knock on the door caught her off guard.

Assuming one of Daddy's customers awaited her, she hurried to open the door and not disturb the baby.

Stepping out onto the porch, she softly blurted out "Patton's not here. He's gone to the store."

Looking into a man's eyes, Lila heard him say "Good. It's you I wanna see."

Lila stood speechless. Their eyes met just like earlier that day. However, this time the gaze wasn't deterred by Daddy's voice. The man reached out and gently touched her face. She jerked her head away and stepped back into the cabin, turning her back toward her visitor. The eager young man followed, crossing over the wooden threshold, gently pushing the door shut behind him.

"This is wrong." Lila's trembling voice whispered, overwhelmed by his touch. The sound of her voice forced him closer. She felt his breath on the back of her neck and smelled the after effects of the moonshine he drank earlier.

Taking Lila by the shoulders, he slowly turned her toward him. She looked down toward the dusty floor, wanting to push him away, but weakened by her passion. Unable to resist the warmth of his touch, she allowed him to draw closer. The silent desire within her became deafening, the cries of her conscience no longer heard. She looked up into his longing eyes and embraced him without restraint.

The squeak of the old cast iron bed she usually shared with her husband, confirmed passion as victor.

Lila crossed the threshold of adultery that day and it soon became a way of life for her. Daddy had many customers that spent time with Lila while he was away. Some of them were married, with families of their own. However, the more moonshine they drank, the prettier Lila became. Soon she gave birth to a third son, Blake Allen. No one was ever sure of who fathered the child, and gossip spread like wild fire on a hot windy day.

Daddy seemed oblivious to the happenings at home while he stayed late at the store, talking and smoking cigarettes. The moon shining business increased all the more and Lila stopped arguing with him about it. All seemed to be going well for Daddy.

However, Lila's shenanigans soon caught up with her. She started having an affair with a man she grew to fear. Spencer and Blake called him "Uncle Bill". Often he'd go berry picking with the three of them and Lila told the young boys to wait in a certain place until she and "Uncle Bill" came back. Sometime later Lila and "Uncle Bill" returned empty handed. My half-brothers realized later in life that what the adults did could hardly be considered "berry pickin". Daddy didn't question the amount of time "Uncle Bill" spent with Lila and the boys.

One day Spencer overheard "Uncle Bill" talking about "gettin' rid of 'em." His mother responded, "No, I could never do that." Not many days after that, Lila left the mountain with "Uncle Bill". The mountain folks thought Daddy told her to leave.

Lila's passion for Daddy burned out like the fire under the old still.

To Daddy everything seemed cold now. He sat down on the same ladder-back chair where Lila had been sitting when she heard that fateful knock on the door. He leaned over and put his head in his large, rough hands.

Daddy, sobbing uncontrollably, revealed his love for Lila, while the old iron bed sat silent in the next room. "What a fool I've been!" He said out loud. He decided his days of drinking had ended. As days passed, Daddy began to ponder how he could possibly raise two young sons by his self. Would the mountain claim them as it had claimed his mother?

Within weeks Daddy sold the property to Fred Yancey, money never exchanging hands between them. He then moved, along with his two young children, into the log shack his father and his two younger brothers shared.

According to Momma, Daddy found employment with a nearby mining company. It proved challenging for two men, two teenagers and two youngsters to survive under one roof. In addition, two of my cousins came to live with them several months. Their momma had died from tuberculosis and their daddy had died as the result of a mine explosion a few years later. They were nearly the same age as Spencer and Blake.

Lila did return to the mountain occasionally to spend time with her sons and help in whatever way she could, but she and Daddy never had a romantic relationship with each other again.

Daddy's life soon took a very surprising turn.

CHAPTER TWO

The Encounter

Patton Compton could often be seen walking up or down the mountain either to go to the store or to work and then make his way back home. While making his trek down the mountainous path late one spring afternoon, he heard the clip clop of what sounded like a horse coming up the curvy mountain terrain.

With her long black hair pulled back in a ponytail and the bottom of her homemade linen dress gathered in front of her, nineteen year old Clara Arnold sat astride a bareback old mule. The docile animal slowly made its way up the winding dirt road. When necessary, Clara shifted her weight to maintain her balance. Periodically she leaned her head and shoulders to one side. Spittle splattered in the dirt.

Like any nineteen year old, Clara wanted a home of her own complete with a husband and children. Tired of cleaning and doing laundry for others, she let her mind drift to thoughts of caring for her own family. Lost in thoughts of the handsome man she wanted to meet and marry, she didn't notice the stranger come around the bend in the road.

Taken aback by the sound of a voice, Clara quickly looked up and saw a tall lanky figure in worn clothes and dusty old boots coming toward her. She pulled back on the reins and the mule came to a sudden stop, but the stranger didn't. He kept walking toward her and now stood only a few feet away, with the smell of cigarette smoke permeating his clothes. His dark wavy hair appeared in dire need of scissors. He looked much older than her, but had a handsomeness attached to his slender frame that couldn't escape the eye.

The stranger spoke, "Hello, Miss," looking directly into her soft blue eyes.

With a big lump in her throat, the attractive teenager tried to return the salutation but couldn't. Swallowing hard, the tobacco she'd been chewing slid slowly down her throat. She fought back nausea, managing to say "Goo,- good afternoon."

Clara continued the conversation, feeling very thankful she'd managed to hide the tobacco from the tall stranger, "I don't think I ever saw you 'round here before," she commented.

"My name's Patton, Patton Compton, divorced with two boys to raise and I need somebody to help take care of 'em, along with three others livin' in the cabin. We need somebody to cook and do laundry. That sorta thing." He informed her.

Skeptical as to whether or not he was telling the truth, the blossoming young woman didn't mention her name to him knowing he could be just another mountain man looking for a little excitement away from his wife. Nonetheless, Patton

Compton, being so pleasing to the eye, offered a fair amount of temptation.

"Well, nice to meet ya', Mr. Compton. I better get on home," responded Clara, kicking the mule in the sides with her worn canvas shoes. The animal started moving leisurely up the road.

The stranger walked on in the opposite direction, his ears attuned to echoes bouncing from one side of the mountain to another seeking an escape, to no avail: *"I am bound for the promise land. Oh, who will come and go with me ....I am bound for the promise land"*. In a peculiar way, her words offered hope.

Clara's mind wandered again, but this time not to the kind of man she wanted to marry. Instead, she thought about the kind of men she knew. They drank and ran around on their wives. She saw plenty, while helping some of her neighbors for a few dollars a week. However, she knew better than to say anything. She kept quiet, even though some of them flirted with her. With her shapely frame and large breasts, she knew she could have just about any of them she wanted. Nonetheless, she was praying and trusting God to put the right person in her life, saving herself for the man she wanted to marry. In spite of that, her mind soon drifted again to thoughts of Patton Compton. Suppose he was telling the truth? Suppose he really did need somebody? She needed to get away from her abusive alcoholic father and maybe, just maybe, they could help each other.

Shortly after arriving home, Clara quickly lost her thoughts in the tasks at hand. She helped her older sister, Sarah, prepare the evening meal and together they carried water from a nearby spring. With the dirty dishes washed and the old dusty wood floor free of debris, the two sisters walked through the house and out onto the long front porch. They sat down on a swing their father had made in between times of getting intoxicated. Two large chains coming from the ceiling and attached to the swing assured its safety. As the swing began to move slowly back and forth, Clara found her thoughts once again with the stranger she'd met earlier.

"Sarah, you ever met Patton Compton?" she asked her sister.

"No, can't say as I have, Clara, why?"

Clara glancing at her sister, responded, "I met him today. I think he lives pretty close and needs some help with two young'uns. His wife left." Pausing, Clara continued "Well, that's what he said anyhow." She had no intention of telling her sister about his dark wavy hair or how handsome he looked.

Sarah, interrupting Clara's thoughts about dark wavy hair, answered "I'll go with you in a few days to see if we can be of help."

Clara knew Sarah would do as she said. Drinking and carousing didn't stand in the way of the mountain folk being kind to one another.

"Thank you, Sarah," Clara told her sister.

Tossing and turning in her bed that night, Clara allowed tantalizing thoughts of the stranger to steal her rest.

Two days later the sisters set out on foot up the winding dusty road, used mostly by horses. They carried what few personal belongings they owned in a brown paper bag, just in case they decided to stay. They soon arrived at their destination.

"This is where that old man lives, Clara. Are you sure we're at the right place?" asked Sarah.

"I'm sure this is it." responded Clara matter-of-factly, trying to hide her doubt.

The two young ladies proceeded cautiously up the wobbly steps. The wooden porch seemed sturdy in spite of rotting floor boards. A little hesitant, Sarah knocked on the weathered door. An elderly gentleman swung the door open. Two young boys playing barefoot on the wood floor looked up. Voices could be heard in the distance. Patton stepped out from another room. "Oh, come on in," he said, walking toward them. "This is my father, Whitten and my brother, Collin," he remarked while closing the door. He then turned his attention back to the guests, "and that's Spencer and Blake there on the floor," he said, peering toward the boys.

The elderly gentleman gently waved the back of an open hand toward a dark soiled couch and asked, "Would you ladies care to sit down?"

While taking advantage of the offer, Clara introduced herself and her sister. "My name is Clara Arnold and this is my sister, Sarah" she said. She noticed a cast iron cook stove in the adjacent room with a dishpan full of dirty dishes near it. A pile of clothes filled the corner of the room where the two sisters sat. The bed in another corner showed signs of needing fresh linen. The smell of cigarette smoke and an overcooked meal hung heavy in the air.

Sarah eyed the two children playing on the dirty wood floor, their clothes almost as black as their feet. The dark streaks across their faces revealed it had been some time since they came in contact with water. She wondered how well the boys knew hunger.

A teenager came through the door and introduced himself as Ralph Compton, Patton's brother. He walked on into the kitchen.

Clara glanced at her sister. Sarah's dark brown eyes darted around the room. The sound of Clara's worn shoe sole hitting the floor while she moved her foot up and down broke the silence.

Abruptly, Sarah spoke, "If you like we'll stay." It seemed better to her than going back to the life they knew.

With the offer gladly accepted, Patton informed them, "The pay's not much, but you'll get a bed and some food."

The two young women found dried beans and potatoes in a pantry. A closer look rewarded them with some corn meal. Informed about cold milk in the springhouse, they prepared the family a meal.

"Sarah, maybe we should've just gone back home," Clara whispered to her sister, while stirring cornmeal and milk together.

"I don't think so. They seem real nice. I know it's a lotta work, but it'll get better," Sarah assured her sister.

The eight of them gathered around a long wooden table the men had constructed out of scrap lumber. Clara observed large spaces between the boards, no doubt left there deliberately to make the table wider. After Patton giving thanks, the men and boys hardly looked up during the meal.

Patton remarked "This sure is good!" spooning brown beans from a chipped bowl.

"It sure is!" his father agreed, periodically taking a drink of milk from a pint canning jar.

With appetites satisfied, the men walked outside and the two young women soon had the dishes put away and the kitchen in order.

A large pan of warm water removed from atop the cook stove, together with lye soap and a little scrubbing, cleansed the crusted dirt from Spencer and Blake. A bath, a full stomach and clean bed linen assured the boys of a good night's sleep.

After reading several chapters from a worn Bible, Whitten blew out the flame dancing atop a nearly empty oil lamp. Ready for a night's rest, he pulled an aging homemade patchwork quilt up close around him and closed his eyes.

Sarah and Clara, exhausted, fell asleep on a soft feather mattress.

Within a few days, the two ladies had all the beds changed and laundry done. Water had been carried from the spring, with the help of the two older boys. Two weeks passed and Sarah decided to go home, leaving her sister to care for the family in need.

"Clarie, would you please hand me some more of that cornbread?" Patton asked, as the family sat around the long table eating supper one evening.

"Sure," said Clara, passing the plate of corn bread to him. Her hand brushed against his and their eyes met. They continued to eat in silence.

Later, after washing the dishes, Clara walked outside. Lost in thought, she was startled by a noise behind her. She turned and saw Patton coming toward her, much like the time they first met. A conversation started between them and time went by quickly. They agreed to continue their conversation at another time.

Clara began to look forward to her time alone with Patton. They spent as much time as they could together in the weeks following. Clara soon realized she'd fallen in love.

Patton Compton and this young lady, Clara Arnold, had been attracted to each other from the first time they met. However, being twelve years her senior, he had no intentions of taking advantage of the young woman. Clara had no intentions of losing her virginity until married. However, Mother Nature took advantage of the small space of the four room shack and Clara found herself in the arms of the stranger she met while chewing tobacco.

And so began a relationship between Clara Arnold and Patton Compton, my mother and father.

Luther Patton Compton and his wife, Clara

CHAPTER THREE

Life in the Shack

Uncle Collin moved to Maryland and later, joined the Navy at the age of seventeen. He took a bride, Grace Dunbar, after he got out of the Navy and they moved back to Virginia, but not to the mountain. Not long after that, Uncle Ralph married a young woman named Lectie Horn and they settled on Black Top Mountain.

Two less occupants in the weather beaten old log shack contributed little to make it more comfortable for those it still housed. The dilapidated shack consisted of two rooms upstairs and two downstairs. Mercifully holding decaying boards in place, it offered what comfort it could afford.

The log shack had a porch downstairs and a balcony upstairs, with missing railings and grey, sagging boards. Obviously, they had not escaped the fierce storms that ascended on Black Top Mountain. Nonetheless, these additions made it impossible for the surrounding mountains to hide their majestic beauty in the fall, but the hardships of winter tainted the splendor of snowcapped trees.

Snow, driven by wind, along with cold temperatures, lacked compassion for the vulnerable occupants of the shack. Layers of clothing offered no threat to the chill in the air. Strong gusts of wind pushed snow through the cracks between the logs.

A blanket of white on the bed made it necessary for Momma to shake the bed covers before climbing beneath the cold quilts. Often coats could be seen stretched over the quilts to battle the cold. Waking up to a fresh blanket of snow on the bed revealed the wind had stalked in the night.

Wood gathered provided fuel for the fire burning in two stoves. The fire in the cook stove not only cooked meals, but offered warmth as well. Finding wood small enough to keep the fire burning in the cook stove proved a difficult task. The "pot belly stove" in the next room consumed large amounts of wood.

Carrying water up the steep mountainside became a necessary part of daily life, along with gathering wood.

When the long cold winter was finally over, Momma thought her chores would be less demanding. Gardening seemed more inviting than gathering wood in the boisterous wind. Nevertheless, the days seemed to get longer and the nights shorter. Momma soon realized she would give birth. She wondered how Daddy would take the news.

Momma had tossed and turned in the bed every night trying to think of the right words to use to inform the man she loved about their baby. Would he tell her to leave? Would he be excited? Should she not tell him at all? She knew he had to find out sooner or later.

It was getting dark outside and Daddy still wasn't home. Momma knew he'd come home hungry, so fried potatoes, pinto beans and cornbread awaited him. He arrived shortly after the darkness had pushed out the light, making it even harder to ascend the steep slope leading to the shack.

After Daddy ate his meal, he made his way up the narrow steps toward the bedroom him and Momma shared.

Momma finished the dishes, taking her time, secretly hoping Daddy would be asleep when she got to the bedroom. If so, she would have an excuse not to tell him about the baby right now. But how long could she put it off with her belly already slightly protruding?

"Clarie, what took you so long? I thought you's going to stay up all night."

"Patton, you know cleaning up takes time," answered Momma.

After sliding beneath the covers, Momma turned on her side toward Daddy and rested her head on her fist. Propped up on her side with her elbow bearing her weight, she stared at Daddy, trying to muster up enough courage to tell him about the baby. The belligerent screech of a limb blowing against the tin roof above them demanded to be heard.

"Clarie, why are you starin' at me?" His forhead wrinkled.

"Sorry, uh-h, Patton," Momma stammered.

Daddy reached out to hug Momma, but she refused his embrace, now determined to tell him about the baby, no matter how he felt.

"What's wrong? You're acting awful strange."

"Patton, I have to tell you somethin'," Momma said matter-of-factly.

"What is it, Clarie? Are you alright?" Daddy's forehead no longer wrinkled. Instead, a serious look came across his face.

"Yes, I'm okay. I'm going to have a baby," Momma softly blurted the words out. Finally he knew about the baby! What would come next?

Daddy turned over in the bed and faced the wall.

Momma asked "Well, are you happy?"

Daddy responded "Let's go to sleep."

Momma blew out the oil lamp on the stand beside the bed. In the darkness, she heard Daddy snoring. Tears trickled down her face. Nothing! He said nothing about her unborn child! She, at least, wanted him to accept her and her child. She had no idea how he felt! Was he unable to express his feelings? Would he ask her to leave in the morning? Momma had nightmares interrupting her much needed rest. She envisioned herself walking off the mountain in the dead of winter with her newborn child and nowhere to go. Daylight brought relief revealing her worst fears had not come to pass.

Daddy never mentioned Momma leaving. He never mentioned them getting' married, either. The months went by and neither said a lot about the baby. However, Momma's protruding abdomen made it impossible to forget the tiny infant in their future.

"Patton, can you carry in some wood for me?" Momma asked Daddy.

Only a few small sticks of kindling remained in the square wood box sitting in the corner, behind the cook stove. Momma secretly wished Daddy had motivation to do without being asked.

Momma grabbed the straw broom, leaning in the corner behind the door, and began to sweep up dust the wood left behind. A piece of paper sufficed as a dustpan. The short pieces of straw the broom left on the floor reminded Momma of the need for a new broom. Oh, if only she had one of those fancy things she had seen at the store and a new broom to go with it! It would be so much easier to sweep dirt up. No use to dream about new brooms and fancy gadgets. Momma had other needs to be met, especially with a baby on the way.

Momma allowed her thoughts to wander while going about daily chores. She mused about her life turning out much different than she'd planned. She had no control over her circumstances now. It was too late now to go back home. She knew her family would not accept the baby. And the baby! Would she have a son or a daughter? What would she name it? How would the man she loved respond to another mouth to feed? Breastfeeding was the only option if she wanted her baby to live. She knew the canned milk on the store shelf could not be afforded along with the cigarettes Daddy smoked. She wished he would quit smoking, so he could provide more for his family.

The little fetus growing inside Momma's womb often woke her up at night with its squirming. The squirming soon had a squall attached to it—Maggie Marie, born March 8, 1944, had all the makings of a perfect baby with thick black hair and sparkling blue eyes.

CHAPTER FOUR

Another, Then Another

Daddy had a daughter he seemed very proud of. He smiled and talked to her while her tiny fingers wrapped around his thumb. She slept nestled close to Momma, making it easier to feed her when she awoke in the night.

Maggie began to roll over, eventually lifting her weight up on her knees and then crawling. Long before Maggie began to walk, Momma knew she was pregnant again.

"Patton, I guess you don't need me to tell you I'm pregnant again," Momma said.

Daddy barely glanced up from the table as he took another bite of cornbread. "Nothin', we can do about it, Clarie".

"Patton, I think it's time we got married," continued Momma.

Daddy kept eating his cornbread and milk as if he hadn't heard what Momma said.

Suddenly Daddy pushed his empty bowl back away from the edge of the table and stood up. With one leg across the wobbly bench he'd been sitting on, he looked up at Momma and remarked, "Clarie, I'll set it up." Balancing his weight on one foot, he threw his other leg across the bench and abruptly walked out the door.

Momma knew they were doing the only thing they could do. She wished it would happen quickly before her belly grew any more.

Momma sat on the edge of the bed holding the light blue dress with lace trim around the top. She'd never thought about it being her wedding dress. Her mind wandered back to her days of housecleaning for others. She thought about the woman that gave her the dress. "I can no longer wear this, Clara. Do you want it?" the kind lady had asked her. Momma tried not to sound eager with her response, knowing the lady could still wear the dress. It was the prettiest dress she'd ever had! She'd been saving it for a special occasion and felt thankful she had something so nice to get married in.

"Clarie, are you ready?" Daddy's voice startled Momma and she hurriedly slipped the dress over her head. She pulled hard on it trying to pull it over her belly. It felt tight, but she knew she couldn't hide her condition, even with loose clothes. Nevertheless, her radiance lit up the room as she entered.

Momma stood beside Daddy in front of the Justice of the Peace. Daddy's handsomeness couldn't hide that day! Dressed in a white shirt and suit coat, he promised Momma he would love her, take care of her and be faithful so long as they both lived. Momma made the same promises to Daddy and they were pronounced husband and wife.

My oldest brother, Benjamin Elmer, graced the world on March 17, 1945, a little more than a year after Maggie. Momma didn't feel ashamed now, knowing she was a married woman. This was not the way she pictured her life. With nothing else to do, she stayed and cared for her two children. Thankful, Daddy had married her, she did all she could to be a good wife.

Momma couldn't understand why her new husband stayed late at the store, offering little assistance with the two babies. Did he not care? Was it another woman? Did he even love her? Momma felt alone.

Maggie slept in the same homemade crib Spencer and Blake had slept in. Momma placed it beside her bed. Ben spent his nights snuggled next to Momma. Grandpa slept on a fold out bed in the living room where the pot belly stove sat in the middle of the floor. The bed served as a couch during the day. Spencer and Blake shared the other bedroom upstairs with Uncle Lake, Grandma's brother.

April 21, 1946 couldn't have been a more perfect day for some of the mountain folk to gather in a nearby cemetery to hold an Easter sunrise service. The sun made a grand entrance over the mountaintop just in time to join the celebration.

While folks gathered in the cemetery to shout praises, Naomi Wood gathered everything she would need to assist Momma in childbirth.

The pains, now more intense, came closer together. Momma felt the hard rough wood cutting into her back. Beads of moisture escaped her weak frame and congregated on her forehead. "Oh, God, please help me," Momma cried to no avail.

"Won't be much longer, now, Clara" informed the midwife. "One more push!"

Daddy, pacing the floor in the living room, wondered when his wife's suffering would end. Would it be another son? Another daughter? Would it be healthy? His thoughts were interrupted by the cry of an infant, he raced into the bedroom.

A tiny infant lay on the bed wrapped in a sheet soiled with blood. He quickly helped Momma up from the floor and into the bed beside her newborn baby.

Naomi Wood took the baby gently from the bed.

"Are you alright, Clarie?" Daddy questioned.

"I'm ok, Patton," Momma barely got the words out. She closed her eyes, still holding tight to Daddy's hand as if expecting another pain to arrive. Daddy took his other hand and determinedly pushed the wet hair clinging to her forehead away from her round face.

The baby's cry became louder. The baby, now washed and wrapped in what remained of a homemade quilt, soon nursed by its mother's side.

Daddy leaned forward to look at his fifth child.

"What is it, Clarie?" Daddy inquired.

"It's a girl, Patton," Momma informed him, watching a broad smile break out across his face.

The sound of rusty hinges resisting the weight of a door distracted the young couple.

Daddy turned to see Uncle Lake standing behind him. "What a pretty little thing," he remarked, "I heard you say it's a girl. I think you should name her Easter, Easter Christine."

"That's fine with me," whispered Momma.

Momma heard the splash of water hitting the wood floor, followed by the sound of the bedroom door closing and footsteps fading in the distance.

Momma closed her eyes and drifted off to sleep.

A few memories from

Christine Saunders

CHAPTER FIVE

Boys, Boys, Boys

Just sixteen months after I was born, I had another brother, Robert Luke. We called him Luke.

Clara holding Luke

Blackberries hung in clusters in a patch near the shack.

Momma asked Uncle Lake, "Would you mind watching these young'uns' while I go get some blackberries?"

"Why, I sure will!" responded Uncle Lake.

"It shouldn't take too long," Momma assured him.

Momma picked up a galvanized beat-up peck bucket and walked out. She could hear Ben crying on the other side of the door.

Obviously pregnant again, Momma walked toward the fence standing between her and the blackberries. Pushing down on the last two strands of sagging rusty barbed wire, Momma carefully leaned down and put first one foot, then the other, through the fence. Then she retrieved the bucket and approached the blackberries.

Momma knew she needed to hurry. However, the much needed seasonal fruit was plentiful and hard to leave behind. And, besides, she almost had the peck bucket full. Hurriedly, she kept picking berries until they filled the bucket.

Not wanting to spill the berries, she cautiously carried them toward the fence *now* standing between her and the shack. Were her babies alright? Was Ben still crying? Was Christine hungry? Would Luke wake up before she got back?

Once at the fence, Momma carefully sat the bucket of berries on the other side. Then she pushed down two strands of the old barbed wire again and put one foot on the other side of the wire. "I'm almost home," she thought. She quickly raised one foot to put it through the fence. When she did, the other foot slipped! The rusty barbed wire cut deep into her legs, as her weight hit the ground beneath the fence. She lay on top of the barbed wire, afraid to move, not wanting any more of the fence's wrath. Then Momma realized she had sharp pain in her abdomen.

Momma pushed her weight up with her elbows, got a hold of the leaning fence post and got both feet on the same side of the fence. With pain nearly unbearable, she managed to get back to the shack while clutching the bucket of berries, determined to feed her children. Uncle Lake realized her dilemma and insisted she lay down.

Within hours, Momma miscarried the baby. While trying to help four of her children, she'd lost one. She had grown to love the little life growing inside her, but she didn't have time to worry about her loss, with four young children to care for.

Momma had another little heart beating inside her womb not many months after the miscarriage, but that was the first year in five that she did not give birth. I was nearing my third birthday when Toby Edward came along. Fifteen months later Jacob Scott appeared. When Jacob was born is about as far back as I can remember things. I remember seeing Sawyer Michael when he was a baby. I thought too many babies was showing up on the place. Then Leon Wallace showed up! I didn't know why they kept being boys. That was September 1952 and I could count to eight, but I had to use my fingers on both hands.

At the age of fifteen, Spencer started working for a local mining company, though it meant dropping out of school and lying about his age. He opened a charge account with the same store where Daddy wasted time gallivanting.

Momma sent Maggie, Ben and me to that same store sometimes to get groceries on a list and tell them we wanted to put it on Spencer's account. We asked the nice man at the store to help us read Momma's writing. Sometimes, she just drew pictures if she couldn't spell the word.

When we got to the big counter with all our groceries, my mouth always watered for one of those Mint Juleps in a big glass jar with a wooden lid on it. I knew I couldn't have one though, because it wasn't on the list. One time we had groceries in a brown bag to carry home and walked almost to the door when the nice man hollered for us. We turned around and he was pulling the wooden lid off the big glass jar. We walked back to the counter as fast as we could while still carrying the groceries. He reached into the big glass jar and pulled out three Mint Juleps. He said we could have them. We were so excited! We kept thanking him until we closed the door behind us. On the way back up the mountain, we talked about how nice that man had been.

Momma wasted no time getting the groceries out of the bag. She took something in one of the cans and mixed it up with water. She poured it in two baby bottles for my little brothers, Sawyer and Leon, to suck on. She taught me how to mix it and let me hold Leon and feed him. He was like caring for a real doll. I was so excited to hold a baby! I felt like a big girl, knowing I'd soon be seven years old.

It didn't seem long after Spencer started the job with the mining company that he decided to leave the mountain and seek a life elsewhere. He finally settled in Lancaster, Pennsylvania. I missed him a lot. He told me stories sometimes.

I didn't think we'd get to go back to the store anymore, so we wouldn't get any more Mint Juleps. Then one day Momma up and sent us back to the store, but the nice man didn't offer us a Mint Julep that time. Momma told us Aunt Nan gave the nice man at the store enough money to get the groceries on the list. By this time Dean Warner had been added to our family. We had to get some more of that canned milk. I thought if we didn't have to buy all this canned milk, I could get a Mint Julep.

I could tell Momma was real upset with Daddy one day when he didn't go to work. She told him he'd have to go find some work somewhere. She said "Patton, you shoulda knowed better than to go chasing a dog on your lunch break!" Daddy then said to Momma "Well, I just wanted to see what the dog had treed. I didn't know it was gonna take so long."

After that I often saw Daddy sitting on the rock wall erected outside the store. He finally did go to work for the railroad.

Daddy's sister, Aunt Nan, sent money every month to the store owner so Momma could keep the charge account to buy much-needed groceries. Aunt Nan left the mountain to seek treatment for Tuberculosis. After regaining her health she found a well-paying job at the treatment center. Since she remained single, it afforded her the means to help Daddy and Momma. However, Daddy often charged cigarettes to the account, so his sister told the store proprietor exactly what the money could be used for.

Momma thanked a man called Jesus for taking care of us.

CHAPTER SIX
Easter Christine, Lookin' Back

Grandpa became ill and added to Momma's responsibilities. Maggie and I helped as much as we could. Washing diapers and dealing with maggots in the summer time became part of our daily routine. Ben and Luke helped us carry water from a spring. I usually didn't have much left in my bucket when I finally got back to the shack. Looking back now, it seems like a lot for four children under the age of ten to accomplish, but we did it.

The dishes needed to be washed every day, too. I stood on a chair to wash the dishes while Maggie helped care for the babies. There seemed to be a lot of both dishes and babies. I had to be careful and not fall. At least, that's what Momma told me. I thought she didn't want me to break one of those glass bowls we mixed cornbread and milk in.

Three short months after Grandpa became ill, he succumbed to his illness and some neighbors carried him out in a homemade pine box to rest beside Grandma. The mountain had claimed another victim, never allowing Grandpa access to a life outside its bounds.

Momma, even with her big belly, stripped the covers fast-like off of Grandpa's bed and washed them on the wash board. I wondered why she hurried so, but I knew Momma didn't have time for questions. I tried to talk to her once and she told me to go play, after asking if me and Maggie got all the diapers washed. I knew I was getting bigger because, if I stood on my tiptoes, I could reach the old clothesline wire, stretched between two trees out back. I really thought it was about time for me to find out how all those babies got on the place. Maggie just kept telling me I'd find out someday.

Later that day, Daddy came home and helped Ben and Luke drag the mattress upstairs. I heard my little brothers arguing at night because they didn't have enough room in the bed, so I thought they would get the extra bed and I'd still have to sleep with Maggie. I was right.

With Grandpa gone and my two half-brothers on their own, the rickety benches on each side of the long wooden table still lacked space for everyone to be seated at mealtime. Me, Ben and Maggie sat on the dirty floor boards while eating brown beans from off a pot lid, sufficing as a plate. We shared milk that filled a Mason canning jar. We were hungry and thankful for food anyway we could get it, never having seen a glass plate. Momma did have the glass bowls in the cabinet, though. I always pushed my finger all the way around the top to see if any little pieces of glass were missing. I hardly ever got a bowl with pieces gone. I guess Momma saw me doing that and didn't want me to get cut. Anyway, I still hoped I might get one sometime.

Daddy never seemed to be home much during the day, but showed up at bedtime. We never had an extra mattress, so him and Momma always had to sleep in the same bed. Maggie said they were supposed to anyway. I never stayed overnight anywhere so I didn't know how other mommies and daddies slept.

Sometimes Daddy didn't look happy when I saw him sitting on the rock wall outside the store at the foot of the mountain. When I got off the school bus I'd run and hug him before us young'uns started up the mountain toward home. It seemed like it took a long time to get home. I heard Daddy say one time that we lived about two miles from the store. I didn't know what he meant by two miles, but knew it must be a long way, because I was completely wore out by the time I got home.

It was not only a long way, but steep, too. One time Luke slid over the bank as we were walking down off the mountain to catch the school bus. He ran a big snag of some sort in his knee. He looked like he was hurt real bad, but we couldn't help him. We went on to school and he went back to Uncle Ralph's house and Aunt Lectie got the snag out and bandaged his knee before he went on home.

It seemed like every few months a new baby showed up, but, of course, it was longer than that. Maggie said it had to be at least nine months between them. Momma's belly would get real big just before it happened.

One time Maggie playfully pulled a chair back just as Momma went to sit down. Momma later got real sick and had to go to bed. Maggie told me Momma lost a baby. I thought maybe they found it when I saw Daddy carrying something wrapped up in his arms. Whatever it was, he took it out behind the house and didn't bring it back. They never found the lost baby and I wondered if somebody else was taking care of it. Maggie told me that man Jesus was. That's the same man Momma talked to a lot. We heard a lot about Him at the church we walked to sometimes. He must be somebody awful special, but I thought He should just give us back the baby. However, I knew Momma probably didn't mind sharing.

I remember one August day being exceptionally hot. Daddy asked us to go and play under the apple tree below the house. Maggie and I were told to take care of one year old Dean and two year old Leon. We obeyed though only nine and eleven years of age. As the smaller children played in the dirt, little streams of sweat began to run down the side of their small faces. Unable to ignore it, they stopped occasionally to wipe it, leaving black streaks behind. However, the heat didn't deter them from playing with rocks in the dirt.

Ben, Luke, and Jacob played on the crooked limbs of the apple tree, enjoying the tasty green apples it produced.

Watching every step we took to insure stability, we failed to notice Daddy walk out on the front porch.

"Ben, Luke, come 'ere. I got somethin' I want ya' to do." The sound of Daddy's voice caused them to jump off a limb onto the ground and run toward the shack. After having received instructions, the two boys started walking down the steep road leading off the mountain.

"What do you reckon is a going on, Ben?" inquired Luke, using his hand to shield his eyes from the bright sunlight as he looked at his brother.

"I don't know. Sure is somthin' strange, though." responded Ben, "I guess we'll find out soon."

The other three oldest boys continued to play while Maggie and I cared for the two younger ones, assuring their safety.

I watched real curious like as several neighbors came and stayed for only a short time. I got to wondering about why we had so many visitors. I didn't know what a special day this would be for my whole family, though I did know something seemed different about it. I watched as Naomi Wood entered the house. I perceived her to be one of Momma's very best friends; after all, she had been there with Momma when my younger brothers showed up.

Without warning, a blood curdling scream escaped from the walls of the old shack. Then I heard Momma yell "Oh, God, please help me!" In my young mind, I thought Momma faced danger of some sort. However, I knew none of the neighbors would hurt Momma, especially with Daddy there. Then I heard Momma yell again.

I decided to sneak to the window and look in. Quietly I started toward the house in spite of Maggie telling me not to.

"You're gonna get in trouble. You better stay here," warned Maggie.

Ignoring the warning, I determinedly continued on my mission. I spotted an old block of wood beneath the window, perfect for standing on so I could see inside. Very quietly I climbed on the block with one hand against the wall, being careful not to stumble. Finally, able to see inside the room, I saw Momma laying on the floor with a white sheet over her legs. Naomi Wilson stood nearby, alongside Daddy.

Suddenly, my foot slipped and I grabbed the window sill. Daddy turned just as I jumped down.

Frightened, I swiftly ran back to the old apple tree without looking back!

Trying to catch my breath, I told Maggie "Momma's on the floor, Maggie! I think she –she's dying." Then I began to cry.

Maggie put her arm around me, assuring me "Christine, don't cry. Momma will be fine."

"How do you know?" I sobbed," Somethin's wrong with her."

Maggie held Dean, straddled against her hip, with one arm wrapped around the small toddler. She pulled me close with her other arm, as we listened to the screams coming from inside the shack.

"Momma's dying, Maggie," I stated again, wiping both sweat and tears from my eyes.

"No she's not," Maggie responded.

Maggie's assurance didn't sound very convincing to me. I started to cry uncontrollably.

"It's so hot, Maggie. Momma can't get any air laying on the floor!"

"Christine, please don't cry," begged Maggie.

Maggie's next words to me produced a huge smile, replacing my tears. "Momma's havin' a baby, Christine! That's why she's in pain. We may have another brother or it could be a sister this time!"

"Oh, Maggie, do you mean we could have a sister?!" I was real excited now, watching the house while trying to listen to conversation inside. I watched Naomi come out on the front porch and pick up a bucket of water and hurry back inside.

I didn't know this was the way I got all my little brothers. I didn't even know what caused it, but I knew I wanted another sister, if one more baby *had* to be on the place.

After what seemed like hours to us, we watched Naomi Wilson start her trek off the mountain.

"Children, you can come back to the house now," Daddy informed us, after stepping out on the front porch, "I wanna show you somethin."

I ran all the way, arriving at the house first, leaving Maggie to assist our younger siblings. Daddy led me into the next room. Momma held the beautiful baby close to her bosom.

The baby's tiny face felt soft to me as I gently rubbed it. I picked up the baby's small hand. Without looking up, I asked "Is it a sister, Momma?"

Momma reached out and touched my shoulder. "Yes, Christine, it is?"

Maggie came into the room and I couldn't contain my excitement. "It's a sister, Maggie! We got a baby sister! Come and look!"

Stepping back, I let Maggie stand in front of the baby.

Glancing around the room, I looked up at Daddy and asked "Daddy, why is the floor so wet?"

Daddy responded, "Oh, somebody must have spilled some water."

I remembered Naomi getting the bucket of water and made the assumption she spilled it on the floor.

My attention quickly diverted back to my baby sister and I asked another question. "What's her name, Momma? I been thinking a lot about a girl's name and I like Libby! Can we, Momma, can we name her Libby Abigail?"

"Sounds good to me." Momma said in a weak tone.

I don't think Momma really cared about names by this time, just as long as we were all healthy. I'd spent a lot of time thinking about a sister's name, though, in case I ever had another one.

The baby girl became known as Libby.

Ben and Luke soon returned with melted ice cream. I knew Daddy sent them off the mountain so they wouldn't hear all the screaming and hollering that day.

I not only got the sister I wanted that day, but also ice cream. The ice cream tasted good in spite of being melted. It was a rare occasion to get ice cream. It did turn out to be a special day for us all, but I don't think having another baby excited Momma much.

Each morning I jumped out of bed and raced downstairs, eager to help care for Libby.

One night Libby's cries woke me up and I quietly went downstairs to where Libby lay beside Momma. Momma, sound asleep, didn't hear Libby cry. I assisted Libby in finding the nourishment she needed from Momma's bosom. Then I quietly tiptoed back up the steps. I don't think Momma ever did wake up the whole night.

CHAPTER SEVEN

Another Look Back

It was twelve of us siblings born in just fourteen years. By the time Patsy, the youngest, was born I began to understand things a whole lot better and didn't have to use my fingers to count us all.

Maggie told me Momma had lost two babies. I finally understood what that meant, too.

I had a hard time getting all the names right, but I didn't feel dumb because Momma sometimes called me Maggie and then realized I was Christine.

After Maggie's birth, Ben came and later, I entered the world. The fourth child, a boy, became known as Luke. The next baby bore the name Toby. The sixth child, Jacob, would be the same age as Sawyer for six days each year; both born in less than a year. I didn't see how they could be the same age and not be twins, not even for six days. After Sawyer's arrival, Leon came into the world, followed by Dean.

With seven boys, six of them born consecutively, and two girls, I thought the babies needed to stop. I felt I had enough little brothers. I didn't know at that time three more babies would make our family complete.

When Libby was born, I was so excited to have a baby sister and to get to name her! Then another boy baby was born; Reggie Matthew. Fifteen months after Reggie's birth, Momma gazed into the blue eyes of her youngest child, Patsy. With all twelve of us children healthy, Daddy and Momma thanked that man Jesus a lot. He was the same one Daddy thanked for our food. I started thanking him, too, hoping He could hear me.

Momma did all she could to care for us. In spite of a table nearly as scantily clad as the log walls, we did grow, and appeared healthy. If sickness visited my family, it usually spent time with each one before making its departure. None of the mountain folks afforded the luxury of medical attention when in need. Occasionally sickness wouldn't leave the mountain without taking a soul with it. The men would then get together and build a pine box while the ladies prepared the body to be kept in a front room overnight. The next day the corpse filled an empty grave in the nearby cemetery. Sickness always left our house empty handed, with the exception of Grandpa.

Momma talked to that man Jesus a long time when one of us got sick. She said He could drive out the devil and make us well. I guess the devil was in that shadow Momma talked about one time. I heard her tell her friend, Naomi, that the devil was just like a shadow following you around trying to get you to do bad things. She told Naomi that man Jesus would take care of her. I never did see the shadow, but knew Momma had. I did look for it sometimes, though.

Momma got awful sick one time. The road in front of our house never had a car on it, so Momma was carried on a mattress about a half mile to Uncle Ralph's house. Somebody then took her to a hospital in Richlands where she had to have a blood transfusion. One of the neighbors came to our house and put dumplings in our brown beans. We never had that before and they sure tasted good!

Christmas came and went, without any great expectations. We thought we lived too far away for Santa and his reindeer to visit and we never expected gifts. When Daddy came home carrying a large package he picked up at the post office, we knew Aunt Nan sent it. She always gave us something warm to wear and pretty, too. Momma made Apple Stack Cakes and molasses cookies. She tried to make the meal special, but there wasn't much to get excited about. I knew somebody celebrated a birthday, but wasn't quite sure who.

If Daddy managed some way to get a hog, and butcher it, Momma accomplished the art of making every part of it edible with the exception of the squeal. We loved the taste of cooked pork brains. To children that sometimes had only a raw potato to eat for dinner, the cooked brains of a hog seemed worth arguing about.

"I want some first, Momma!" yelled Ben.

Maggie snapped back, "I'm the oldest, I should be first!"

We soon had little to say with a mouth full of cooked pork brains.

With our knowledge limited to that of life on the mountain, we believed the entire world to be like Black Top Mountain. With the exception of a few families which prospered by their investments in the coal mines, most people living in the area lived like we did. We saw cardboard over their windows and took note of their outside johnny house.

I didn't understand why we couldn't visit other people, at least once in a while. I never did ask Momma if I could go talk to somebody else. I didn't know if anybody even wanted to talk to me and didn't really know what to say if they did. I thought my life to be just like everyone else's. I did wonder sometimes what was on the other side of the mountain. We never talked about it.

My family struggled from one day to the next, but I didn't really think so at the time. Momma used what little she had to meet our needs. As far as she was concerned, when something couldn't be used in one way, it could be used in some other way, with very little discarded. Ragged shirts added color to the beds in the form of quilts, but not before the buttons were salvaged. We older kids would sit on the floor beneath old quilting frames, assisting Momma by pushing the needle back through the quilt to her. It made the quilting go much faster and we enjoyed taking turns. I enjoyed doing something besides washing dishes and diapers. I had fun watching the thread disappear. Then we waited for the needle to appear again. Once in a while we got stuck, but it didn't hurt.

Old sheets provided diapers, washed over and over by me and Maggie on the old wash board until some of them fell apart in the water. It made me and Maggie happy when they fell apart, but we didn't say anything about that to Momma. She needed every diaper she could get. In warm weather Maggie and I had to go the old rain barrel at the end of the house and get water. We dipped it out with a small bucket to fill a big tub. Then we dipped the diapers in it. Why, I never saw so much poop! It seemed like more than what I could see when I looked down the hole in the johnny house!

Flour sacks saved became skirts for us girls as Momma sat late into the night sewing. She had a sewing machine and sometimes she made shirts for the boys. I loved my little flowered skirts she made. I liked to help her hold the cloth as it ran across the wooden top and the needle went up and down in rhythm to Momma's foot.

Aunt Nan made it possible for Daddy to buy fifty pounds of dried pinto beans at one time. They filled a burlap sack. Maggie and I sat at the handmade table looking through dried beans for little rocks and bad beans. Sometimes a bean fell through the cracks in the table. Every bean seemed very precious to us.

One time Daddy brought two big black and white coon hunting dogs home with him.

Momma said "Patton, you know you can't keep those dogs. You're taking food from my children to feed them dogs." Daddy took the dogs somewhere. I never saw them again. I thought it would be nice to have a pet, but I guess they would eat a lot and Momma wasn't about to let us go hungry and feed two dogs! I was glad she felt that way about us.

In the smoldering summer heat I watched Momma wipe the beads of sweat from her face when the hoe stopped bouncing off the hard rocky ground. Momma then sang *"I am bound for the promise land...oh, who will come and go with me? I am bound for the promise land"* and talked to that man Jesus a lot while she worked. I thought that shadow must be somewhere nearby. It didn't seem to bother Momma, though, as she spent hours beneath the hot sun planting seeds she had saved from the produce she had gathered the year before. I watched her save those tiny tomato seeds, squash seeds and oblong cucumber seeds. She also saved beans to use for seed. She cut potatoes into pieces and dropped the pieces in the ground. She told me each piece had to have an eye on it. I thought it sure was a funny looking eye.

I knew that man Jesus helped her again as we placed filled Mason jars on the shelf in a cellar and laid sacks of potatoes nearby. I helped Momma put the special lids on the cans of food. I listened close to hear the lids go "pop."

One time Momma grabbed her big belly and dropped the hoe. Soon after that we had another baby to care for. After a few days, Momma returned to the garden and started pulling weeds. She said she would never lose even one of us to the mountain. After she talked to that man Jesus, she said He gave her strength.

Momma sometimes filled a large aluminum pan with corn on the cob and boiled the corn on top of the cook stove. She also cooked large amounts of pinto beans and homemade soup in a large pot so it would be enough to feed us all. I remember a neighbor stopping by one day and after seeing the large amount of corn, he told Momma "Well, Clara, it looks like you're gonna feed a bunch a hogs!" I don't think he knew just how much we did eat and I didn't like being called a hog.

Momma also took milk and made thick cream gravy to add to the potatoes. She also did the same with peas and sometimes corn, after it'd been cut off the cob. She found ways to make the food go further.

Uncle Ralph gave us corn in the winter time. Momma cooked it all day with lye to get the husk off of it. Then she washed it through many pans of clean water. It would be nearly a barrel full when she finished. It lasted several days. I remember coming home from school hungry and eating right out of the barrel!

Momma picked green beans off the vines after they started to turn yellow. She called them the "last pickin' of the season". She pulled threads from the burlap sacks she saved and got a big needle. After she put the thread through the eye of the needle, she began putting the beans on the thread, one by one. Sometimes she let us help. The filled thread was hung up behind the old cook stove. Then she put beans on another thread and hung it from the ceiling. With more than just a few threads of beans

hanging behind the cook stove to dry, we knew
Momma would be sitting a pot of "Leather
Britches" on the table. We could hardly wait to eat
the cooked dried beans!

CHAPTER EIGHT

Nights on the Mountain

After Momma and Daddy moved their sleeping arrangements to the living room, the boys and girls had separate bedrooms.

Another bed in the living room provided a place of comfort for Uncle Lake, as we called him. A nearby homemade crib always held one baby, if not two. Often a drawer removed from a dresser would provide a place for another baby to sleep. Momma always wanted her babies close by.

Momma hardly found time for sleep, with at least one child crying nearly every hour of the day. We soon got used to all the squalling and it didn't bother us at night. After a day of chores, we paid no mind to a baby crying. Most of the time, it was three babies wearing diapers and Momma breast feeding two.

Closing our eyes to rest didn't blind us to the hardships of Black Top Mountain. The boys slept in one room upstairs while I and Maggie slept in the other. Three beds occupied the room the boys slept in. Our small forms sank deep into the bare feather mattresses. Maggie and I slept together, Maggie often pulling me close to keep me warm. In the extreme cold temperatures I would've froze to death if not for Maggie.

The radiant full moon cast an eerie light on the venerable mountain forcing its darkness to take refuge behind the tall timbers.

"Scoot over, Ben. I'm about ready to fall outta bed," complained Toby.

"Oh, you ain't done it." said Ben.

Momma's voice drifted up the stairwell, "Boy's hush up and go to sleep."

"But, Momma, Ben and Luke won't share the bed," whined Toby.

Another familiar voice entered the situation. "Young'uns, I'm not tellin' you again to go to sleep and stop arguing. Ben, you and Luke share the bed!"

Silence followed Daddy's remarks, because my brothers knew there'd be big trouble if they didn't obey.

"Maggie, I gotta go," I shook Maggie, tryin' to wake her up.

Maggie turned toward me and then rolled back over toward the wall.

"Well, go on if you gotta go. I don't need to."

I let Maggie know I didn't approve of her decision to let me go out alone." I see you don't care if somethin' gets me!"

The old steps creaked as I made my way slowly down them.

On more than one occasion, during the night, the screeching of the rickety wooden steps could be heard as one or more of us made our way down the dark stairway and outside. The familiarity of the worn path leading to the outside johnny house deemed any light unnecessary. Us frequent visitors never knew where the Sears Roebuck magazines originated from, but we were thankful the old johnny house stayed well stocked.

I often laid awake in bed trying to fight off the urge to pee, knowing how cold that old wooden floor would feel under my feet. That only worked for a short time and then I slid my feet into flip flops and put on an old coat stretched across the bed. Once outside I pulled the coat tighter; a feeble attempt to divert the frigid temperatures.

The Lightning bugs lit up the warm air in the summer. Nonetheless, it could be a little spooky anytime, especially if the moon refused to offer its assistance. Sometimes I ran back to the house as fast as I could. I never did tell anyone how scared I felt.

Indoor plumbing and electricity never graced the log shack, though it would have made life less demanding. We never even thought about such luxuries, not knowing they existed elsewhere.

CHAPTER NINE

Good and Evil

Daddy talked to us about that man Jesus. At times some of us sat on his lap while others stood nearby, listening to Daddy's instructions, "Be honest, do what is right and be kind to others."

I straddled his knee, as if riding a horse, listening intently as he continued. "There's two roads in this life. One is straight and is good for traveling to walk along with Jesus. It will lead to a great and wonderful place to spend eternity, a place called heaven. I want all my children to go to heaven."

Wide-eyed, we continued to listen as Daddy spoke, "The other road leads to a bad place. It's crooked, rocky and hurts your feet. Don't follow this road. It leads to a place called hell. This road is created by Satan, the devil. He sets up road blocks any way he can to get you off the good path."

I understood what Daddy meant. Sometimes I did wrong and knew it. Plain and simple, Daddy explained the need to obey our parents. Grateful for parents who talked to that man Jesus, I tried hard to do as I'd been told. I knew Momma saw the devil and he looked like a shadow. I didn't want to see him. Seeing a big shadow always scared me.

Grandpa was a preacher, like the one at the church Maggie and I went to sometimes. However, I never did see Grandpa go to church. I guess he was too old. Daddy said Grandpa used to be a circuit rider. He told us Grandpa traveled around to different houses and prayed for the sick and married people and things like that. I listened real close and I found out that talking to that man Jesus is called "prayer." I never saw anybody get married and I didn't understand how Grandpa could be married to so many people. I thought it'd be fun riding around meeting people. Daddy said Grandpa rode a horse.

Grandpa wouldn't tolerate cussing under his roof and we knew it. He made that very clear to all and Daddy encouraged the teaching of his father and tried to instill it in us. I remember a time when Toby forgot what Daddy taught us and we thought hell awaited us all, even though we didn't even know where it was. Daddy said it was bad and I didn't want to go.

In the summer heat we found it to be a little cooler under the trees, so we played on a steep ridge on the side of the mountain. Seeing some big rocks, we decided we could roll them off the mountain and watch them bounce down the steep incline. Finding some rather large rocks on top of the ridge, we pushed them down the side of the mountain. Ben said they'd been there long enough. I didn't know how he knew that and didn't ask him.

Some good neighbors lived at the bottom of the ridge. I didn't think we should roll the rocks toward their house.

"What if we kill that sweet lady that lives there?" I asked.

"You worry too much, Christine," Maggie told me.

After that I kept quiet. We continued to roll loose rocks off the mountain watching them bounce down the steep incline, none of them hitting the house.

Toby pushed and pushed on one rock and couldn't get it to move and finally said "The damn thang won't move!"

I could hardly believe what I heard.

"Toby! The devil will get us for sure. You know what Grandpa always says!" shouted Ben. "We better get on home!"

We made our way off the side of the mountain and onto a dirt road leading home. We came to a fork in the road and Luke suggested, "Let's go out by Grandpa's ole place. It'll be closer."

Rumors created the image of a haunted house. We entered it once before and made our way up the creaky steps to look at some old books. A black cat jumped out of the chimney. It scared us half to death. We ran home that day as fast as we could go. We never did go back.

I spoke up first "I don't know Luke, you know it's haunted. We better not."

"Oh, it ain't haunted," said Ben. "Come on. We need to hurry."

We quickly made our way up the path pushing' the hanging' tree limbs out of our way as we went. I wondered what the devil looked like. I was so scared I thought I was going to throw up.

Silently, we rounded a curve and the run-down cabin came into view. We neared the shack and the door swung open. A hand appeared and a bucket hit the ground not too far from us. Sure we'd seen the devil's hand, our bare feet beat the path toward home!

We told Momma what happened and she told Daddy when he arrived home. However, he thought it of no use to punish Toby, since we had been so afraid of the devil. I didn't hear Toby cuss again and I never did go back to the old shack. We learned later that some of the mountain folks, using the old shack to play poker, threw the bucket outside.

Most Sunday evenings Maggie and I walked off the mountain heading to church. Sometimes Daddy walked with us. With only the moonlight to guide us, I felt safe as long as I held Daddy's hand. I gripped his hand tight. A worn path formed by our little feet going up and down the mountain directed our steps. I loved hearing about that man Jesus. I started talking to Him a lot.

Daddy sometimes had a flashlight. When we reached the bottom of the mountain, he hid it in a place where we could find it; near a big rock. We walked on to church, but Daddy turned back. Usually, somebody with a vehicle stopped to offer us a ride. Since Daddy didn't own a car, we loved to ride, especially when it was cold outside. When we could, we got the flashlight and used it as we walked back up the mountain alone after the service ended. Sometimes the darkness made me afraid. Maggie told me everything would be all right.

Daddy told us how that man Jesus took care
of him one evening as he walked up the mountain.
He said he stopped at the store late and bought a big
bag of flour and started carrying it home across one
shoulder. He said he didn't know he would see an
enemy while going up the mountain with the flour
on his back. Half way up the mountain, Daddy
heard leaves crunching behind him and turned just
in time to see a shadowy figure coming toward him.
A rock flew through the air and the shadowy figure
ran into the nearby woods. The rock burst the bag of
flour. Daddy kept on walking with what flour he
had left and said he wasn't afraid of the devil. I
thought Daddy might've seen the same shadow
Momma did.

We enjoyed hot biscuits for breakfast the next
morning and never knew who wanted to hurt my
Daddy or why. I was glad that man Jesus helped
him. I thanked Him.

(back row left to right) Christine, Luke, Maggie and Ben (front)Toby

CHAPTER TEN

Listenin' In

Above the narrow, rocky road winding by the log shack stood a rather large locust tree. For Luke and Toby, climbing the tree became part of everyday life during the summer. In spite of Luke being only five years old, he could scamper up a tree like a bear in the wild. So, the two decided to put his skills to the test. The goal was to construct a swing with a long line of cable and an old board. With the cable fisted in his little hand, Luke started climbing, his mind set on walking across the very high, crooked and long limb.

Toby and I stood on the ground staring upward, "Do you think he can do it?" I asked.

"Sure he can. If he does fall, we can catch 'im!" Toby replied confidently.

Without hesitation, Luke crawled on all fours out on the limb, holding a cable tight.

"That's far enough," I informed him. Luke stopped and looked down, resulting in his knees shaking. We were ready to catch him, should he fall. Nonetheless, Luke regained his balance and managed to stretch out on the limb and secure the cable around it.

Luke, being back safe on the ground, helped Toby find a board suitable to attach to the cable. The two soon had a swing finished.

Daddy and a couple of his friends where sitting on the front porch one evening. Daddy had an old pocket knife whittling on a piece of wood trying to pass the time of day. I overheard him talking about us. He referred to me as his *"little sugar foot."*

"They're something else," said Daddy, "my little sugar foot was just a singin' away." He proceeded to tell them about hearing me sing.

I enjoyed singing while the homemade swing swayed back and forth beneath me. *"Give Me That Ole Time Religion"* became my favorite song.

Daddy said he and Momma stood listening from the front porch as I sang *"Gimme me that ole time religion, it will take our salt to heaven."* I always wondered why God wanted our salt.

After some laughter, Daddy continued with another story, "Christine and Luke nearly got killed coming home from school, but the good Lord took care of 'em."

Every afternoon when we got off the school bus at the foot of the mountain, we always turned and watched the bus leave. The steep winding road up the mountain leading to the log shack created dread in us, hungry and tired from a challenging day at school. We knew the way only too well. However, the trek each afternoon still overwhelmed us.

"Come on. Let's go up the old minin' road! Its closer." shouted Luke, walking toward a worn path beside the road.

"Ok," I said as I followed Luke.

"You two better stay with the rest of us," Maggie told us.

In spite of Maggie trying to persuade us not to leave our familiar path, we insisted and the two of us started our journey up an old mining road. The road began to narrow.

I stopped, asking Luke, "Are you sure you know the way?"

Luke, looking back, assured me, "I know exactly where the path ends. Come on." He waved his arm as he turned to continue up the narrow road. I followed close behind him. I felt safe with Luke by my side. Though only seven, he seemed very mature to his eight year old sister.

The two of us continued our climb upward until Luke came to an abrupt halt.

"Shhh," Luke whispered to me. Though I wondered why he had stopped, I didn't speak. The sound of dry leaves crunching made my heart beat faster, but I knew Luke would let no harm come to me. The sound drew closer. We gazed in the direction of the noise. What we saw nearly took our breath away. Just above us on a high bank stood a bobcat growling and revealing his teeth, ready to attack. My heart beat even faster

Luke whispered to me, "I got a knife in my pocket. Don't be afraid. I'll take care of you."

I stood still, paralyzed by fear. However, knowing Luke had a knife in his pocket assured me all would end well. I watched Luke slowly reach down and pick a rock up from off the road. As swift as he could he hurled it at the bobcat. The bobcat turned and ran in the opposite direction.

We hurried home, the log shack a welcome sight. We told Momma what happened. Our experience that day made the walk up the steep winding road less tedious.

"The Lord sure is good, Patton" remarked one of the men with Daddy.

"My little sugar foot nearly got killed another time, too," Daddy told the visitors as they listened intently to his next story.

On this occasion, we had taken a break from our chores. The woods in back of the shack held many mysteries for us, making it a very exciting place to play. Finding bugs, spiders, and frogs became a favorite pastime. Sometimes a garter snake crawling under a log or nearby rock proved a fascinating sight. Finding a big grapevine to swing on increased our excitement something fierce since we loved swinging. Assured of no trees in our way, we younger siblings took turns swinging on the grapevines.

One day, me and Toby became impatient while waiting our turn to swing and we decided to walk deeper into the woods. Toby scampered up a nearby slope. I kept walking slowly, allowing Toby time to catch up to me.

Without warning I felt a sharp pain in my lower back and fell to the ground, dazed. Luke saw what happened and ran toward me.

"She's dead, Toby, you killed our sister!" Luke exclaimed, as he neared me. It sounded like his voice was way off in the distance.

"All I did was throw an old cow skull off the bank. I wouldn't tryin' to kill nobody." Toby was starting to cry. Luke put his arms around Toby offering him comfort, trying to hide the tears forming in his own eyes, as he thought about me. The boys began to sob together, not wanting to tell the rest of the family I was dead.

Through blurred vision Luke saw something unusual. "It can't be," Luke said out loud. Looking over Toby's shoulder he watched as I slowly moved my head from side to side. Quickly pushing Toby to one side, Luke ran to me.

"She's alive, Toby! She's come back from the dead!" announced Luke, as I opened my eyes.

I stood up while Luke held on to me. I felt very dizzy at first. Toby ran and hugged me. We continued to play in the woods until Momma called for us.

Luke and Toby concluded that I didn't die, as first believed. It was a good feeling, though, to think I might have come back from the dead.

None of us told Momma or Daddy about the incident, afraid of the consequences. Toby never threw another cow skull.

Daddy said he overheard us talking and kept quiet. I didn't know he had heard us talking.

"Luke put rabbit stew on the table one evenin'," Daddy continued the conversation with a heroic story and I could tell he was real proud of us.

When winter came, two inches of snow blanketed the ground. That was not only pleasing to the eye, but it pleased us siblings as well. Like any other youngsters, we enjoyed running through the snow, in spite of the cold temperatures. Luke stopped near an old pipe noticing tracks leading into the pipe. A closer look revealed the snow undisturbed at the other end of the pipe. Luke became very excited by the prospect of having cooked rabbit for dinner that evening.

Luke instructed me, "You stand at this end of the pipe and poke a stick in it. When he runs out the other end, I'll clobber him!" Luke planned for the rabbit to run out the end of the pipe where he waited for it. With the mountainous area absent of deer, we both knew *any* meat on the table would taste good.

I used the stick Luke gave me and did what he told me to do. At first, it seemed that rabbit would stay put. Since we were so hungry, we were willing to wait him out. Then, all at once, the rabbit bolted out the end of the pipe where Luke stood waiting for it! Luke, though somewhat startled, prevailed and we ate cooked rabbit that evening.

"Clarie sure can make good rabbit stew," alleged Daddy.

I stopped listening after that so I don't know what else he talked about.

CHAPTER ELEVEN

Buses and Bullies

One day at school when I was real hungry, I sat alone eating a peanut butter biscuit Momma had made me for lunch. I tried to hide out of shame since I couldn't buy the school lunch; not even a carton of milk. But one of the more "well-to-do" children, Annie Grubbs, saw me. When she approached me, I spoke to her and tried to be nice. She didn't speak, but kicked me on the shin, turned and walked away. It made me turn toward the wall and cry while I finished eating my biscuit. Incidents of this kind often happened to us.

We couldn't understand why we was singled out. It made going to school a dread each day for all of us, always wondering if someone would bully us. Sometimes I was made fun of for having only flip-flops on my feet.

One morning Momma gave me a sweet potato
in a brown bag to carry to school for my lunch. I
knew I would be laughed at, so I decided I would
save it until after I got home from school. I quickly
looked for a place to hide the sweet potato. I found
the perfect place, a big log near the bus stop!

"You better hurry," said Toby. "The bus is
comin'!"

I tucked the brown paper bag tight around the
sweet potato and carefully laid it against the log and
out of sight.

I made my way to the back of the bus and sat
down. Maggie sat next to me. Looking out the
window, I thought about how good the sweet potato
would taste after school. I couldn't wait for the day
to end.

The big yellow school bus slowed down and
then came to a stop. I slowly walked behind the
others, trying to go unnoticed. Stepping down, I
heard the United States banner snapping in the
harsh wind. My thin little flip flops cried "flip flop,
flip flop", drawing attention to them. I tried to put

all my weight on the rubber soles at one time, hoping the noise would go unheard, but it didn't. I heard snickering and glanced up, just as I walked through the double doors.

"Good morning, Christine," Mrs. White said.

I responded, while she eyed me from head to toe, "Good morning, Mrs. White."

"Seems a little cool this morning for those flip flops", she continued.

I walked on past without commenting.

"Look at them, would ya'?" Annie loudly blurted out. She and the two girls with her started laughing out loud.

Annie continued, "Hey, you wanna see my new shoes, Christine?!"

Their laughter echoed in my ears while I sat at my desk waiting for class to begin.

I looked around, twisting all the way around in my seat. I spotted a pencil! I ran and picked it up, figuring Mr. Vince had left it there on purpose when he swept the floor that morning. He was a nice man.

The bell rang and I watched the others take their seat at their desk.

I took note of Annie's shoes when she walked past me. They were the same shoes she had been wearing. She didn't get new shoes!

Mrs. White started writing something on the black board. I turned and asked the boy sitting behind me for a sheet of paper. With a long sigh, he reluctantly handed me a piece of paper.

"Thank you," I whispered.

I squeezed my stubby pencil tight, trying hard to hold onto it. I felt real thankful Mr. Vince didn't sweep it up that morning. If he had, I would just be sitting still while everyone else wrote and stared at me.

I turned and saw Ben and Luke writing. I sure was relieved! What about Toby, I wondered? Does he have a pencil? I had no way to know since he was in another classroom. I wished I could give him mine if he didn't have one.

"Christine, you need to turn around and pay attention," scolded Mrs. White.

"Yes mam," I responded in a low voice, feeling my face reddening. Annie and some her friends snickered. I could feel her cold eyes burning into my flesh. I tried to ignore her. Oh, I wished the day would end!

I had to get out of my seat to walk up to see the blackboard, because Mrs. White's boyfriend was there talking to her. At least that's what everybody called him. I didn't understand that because they were both married to someone else. I wished he would stop leaning over Mrs. White's desk and go on home, so I could see the board!

The lunch bell rang and I was glad I'd get to talk to my brothers. I heard Toby and Mark Duncan arguing. I knew Toby would get in trouble again, because he made up his mind he wasn't going to be bullied any longer.

The big door closed behind us. All I could think about was my sweet potato in the brown paper bag. I wished I had brought it on to school even if

Annie did make fun of me. My stomach growled, begging for food.

"I sure am hungry," said Toby.

"Me, too," I said to my brother. "I know Maggie would share if she could."

Maggie had the good fortune of working in the lunch room and getting her lunch free. They wouldn't let her share with us. I wished I could work in the lunch room, but I wasn't old enough.

I and my brothers, along with other children that had no food to eat, had to sit in a big room while the other children ate in the lunch room. I knew Annie would be telling me how good it tasted when I got back to the room.

When lunch ended we were allowed to go back to the room, hungrier than ever. I could hardly concentrate on my work. I kept thinking about my sweet potato.

When the bell finally rang at the end of the day, I walked as fast as I could without getting in trouble.

I took a seat on the bus and peered over the seat in front of me, watching the others get on the bus. I swung my feet back and forth, trying to keep my flip flops attached to them. I heard the folding door at the front of the bus close and soon we were headed home!

I stepped off the bus and ran as fast as I could go to the rock where I hid the sweet potato! There it was! The brown bag, just like I left it! Luke stood looking over my shoulder as I reached down and grabbed the bag. I knew he was every bit as hungry as me!

I opened the bag, then threw it down, wiping my hands on my dress tail.

"What's wrong, Christine? What did you go and do that for? I'm about starved," responded Luke to my actions.

"Ants, Luke, ants!" I shouted, with tears welling up in my eyes.

Luke picked up the bag and hurriedly looked in it. The sweet potato was covered with black ants! Luke slung it over into the woods.

"Luke, if only they didn't treat us so bad at school, I could've took my sweet potato," I told my brother.

Luke exclaimed, "We'll show 'em, we'll show 'em all one of these days! Don't you worry none."

One morning while we were still on the bus, Toby and another boy began to argue. Toby insisted a gallon of bleach is called "bleach," while the other boy insisted it was called "Fleecy White," which was a brand name at the time.

"I'm tellin' you. Its bleach!" exclaimed Toby.

"No, it ain't!" insisted the other boy, "Its Fleecy White."

"I know it is too bleach!" argued Toby. When we stepped off the school bus, they were still arguing. Toby turned to walk away when the other boy shoved him, saying "You know I'm right." That was enough for Toby and he started swinging his fist at the boy. I don't know if the boy believed

Toby after that or not, but he never pushed him again.

The mountain and our situation gave us more distractions than encouragement when it came to learning. The bullying alone made pretending we were in school much more appealing than actually going to school. Never having so much as a crayon or a coloring book, we put our imagination to good use. We would often play softball when we could find a ball to play with. We had an old baseball bat that Ben found in the weeds and when we had no ball, we played tag and hide and seek.

One day we played near a big oak tree not too far from the house, unaware that Momma was standing at the window, watching us play.

The oak tree had large roots on top of the ground branching out in different directions leading down a hill. We used them as "steps". Maggie took Jacob by the hand and led him down the "steps." They were nearly to the bottom when Maggie heard something and glanced to the side and saw a

rattlesnake curled up, ready to strike. She suddenly
realized what she heard was a warning. Maggie
gasped and quickly pulled Jacob back out of harm's
way, just as he neared the snake. We all ran as fast
as we could to Momma.

"Momma. Momma! It's a snake!" Maggie
shouted.

Momma heard us and ran out to meet us.
Upon hearing about the snake, she hurried to a
neighbor's house and asked them to come and kill
the rattlesnake. We stretched it out in the yard that
evening for Daddy to see. He said that man Jesus
had protected his family again.

CHAPTER TWELVE

A Rooster and a Mule

It always proved to be an exciting time for us when we had something special to eat.

One hot summer day, Momma called for Dean to come into the shack. She directed his vision through one of the cracks in the floor of the kitchen.

"Do ya' see that big red rooster under the floor right there, Dean?" She said pointing at a rooster. "I want you to crawl under there and grab him by the legs. I want him for Sunday dinner." Momma knew she always had somebody come by for dinner on Sunday. She would have rather fed us, but never would turn neighbors away from her table.

Dean, being only six years old, responded, "Oh, yeah, Momma, I'll get 'im for ya'."

"You gotta be fast," Momma warned.

"Don't you worry Momma, I'll get 'im," Dean assured her, walking toward the door.

I stood nearby looking down through the cracks in the floor with great anticipation.

Dean slowly crawled underneath the house, being small enough to get under it. The chickens cackled and scattered as though a fox chased them. Dean caught them off guard, grabbing the rooster's legs. It put up a fight, not wanting to become Sunday dinner. His dirty little hand held tight to the rooster as it hit him in the face with its wings. Dean was not about to let go!

The rooster was scalded and plucked. The feathers were saved and used to fill a hand-sewn pillowcase to make a pillow.

The following Sunday, the chicken and dumplin's waited on the stove ready to feed whoever might drop by. I heard Momma say, "Here comes the whole Cox's army," when she heard footsteps on the front porch. Momma knew she needed to get dinner on the table right away. I could tell Momma didn't like to cook extra every Sunday. She had enough to care for without neighbors taking advantage of her. She would never sit down and eat at the table, always afraid it wouldn't be enough food.

Daddy couldn't resist bragging about his wife's cooking. As a result, sometimes each of us only received one bite of the tasty chicken.

An incident not forgotten happened when Momma needed wood during an ice storm. With freezing rain outside, she didn't know what time Daddy would make it home. She became hesitant about sending Luke and I to look for wood while ice quickly accumulated outside. Nonetheless, the wood was a necessity.

Momma called for the two of us and instructed us, "Go borrow the one-eyed mule from Mr. Thompson to pull the ole sled. Go get me some stumps, sticks or whatever else you can find to use for wood."

Luke and I made our way to Mr. Thompson's cabin over on the next ridge. My bare hands ached from the cold. The hard pellets of ice beat against my face as my thin coat began to absorb the moisture.

When we finally reached the neighbor's cabin Luke knocked on the door. It felt good just to stand under a roof without ice showering down on me, even though I was still shivering. Mr. Thompson opened the door, saw us and said, "Come on in, children. You must be freezin'." I guess he saw me shivering.

"Momma sent us to borrow your mule to pull a sled." Luke told the kind elderly man.

"We gotta get some wood," I chimed in.

Mr. Thompson did let us borrow the mule and it pulled the sled up the side of the mountain following a worn path, though difficult on the ice. We managed to keep our footing and soon we were on top of the ridge in a clearing and had the old mule turned around.

Luke and I found what we thought to be a good size stump. With cold feet and gloveless hands we dug it out of the ground. We turned to throw it on the sled just in time to see the sled start sliding forward into the mule's legs. It hit the mule with such force it caused the mule to lose his balance and go backward onto the sled. Once the mule's feet were off the ground and the sled no longer hindered, it began to slide down the hill with the mule on top of it. The sled picked up speed as it went downhill, and was soon out of sight!

"Oh no!" shouted Luke. We were astonished, never seeing anything like that before, thinking the mule would die for sure. We started to run on the ice. My feet were numb and I fell down. Luke turned to help me just as another neighbor, Mr. Honaker, came into view.

"You won't believe what I just saw!" He exclaimed.

Without hesitation Luke responded "Yes, I will! Which way did it go?"

Mr. Honaker led us to where the mule stood in front of the sled. The mule, looking somewhat confused, seemed to be fine. Our kind neighbor helped us get some wood to the house and the stunned mule back to Mr. Thompson. We never borrowed the mule again to gather wood, and we were thankful it survived the sleigh ride.

CHAPTER THIRTEEN

Summer Times

The heavy snowdrifts of winter melted deep
into the earth, rewarding the trees that dared to
stand tall in the boisterous wind with green leaves
to cover their bare branches. They invited us to play
underneath them to relieve us from the sweltering
heat of summer. However, the cool mountainside
did little to calm our imagination. What one of us
didn't conjure up in our mind, another did.

"Look, I found one!" exclaimed Jacob one
afternoon. Those of us playing together ran toward
him to see what he'd found. "It's good n dry, too!"
he yelled.

Ben handed Jacob a long stick. Jacob held the
stick tight with both hands, about six inches from
the ground in front of him. Forcefully, he pushed
the stick into the center of a dried hard cow pattie.
Then he lifted the stick over his head very carefully
and swung as hard as he could, holding tight to the

stick. "There it goes!" he yelled, as the cow pattie flew through the air like a Frisbee.

"Come on, let's go find another one," remarked Sawyer, looking around.

Sticks were important to us. We not only used them to hold cow patty Frisbees but also to write in the dirt. At times, they became trucks in our minds and we drove over roads formed on the ground by our hands. We found many other uses for them as well.

"Here's one!" I shouted.

"It sure is!" Luke said looking up toward the corner of an old shed. "We'll need some long sticks for this one!"

We looked around and each one soon held a stick in their hand. Ben took the stick he held and poked into the corner of the shed. He turned and ran.

"Watch out!" I hollered as I swatted at a wasp coming toward me. The others were trying to kill the wasps now flying around them. "I just got stung, but I'll get 'im!" said Jacob, determined to not let the wasp get away.

Within minutes, nearly all the wasps lay on the ground dead. We took the sticks and searched for another wasp nest to tear down.

We often tied a string to a June bug's leg and let it go, watching it fly as we held to the string. A night light shone out of our imagination as we filled a pint jar with lighting bugs and watched them light up the darkness as we lay in bed. What one of us didn't think of, another one did.

One day Ben thought he had come up with a real good idea.

"I didn't know Grandpa still had these," remarked Ben, holding up a pair of old sheep shears. "I'd like to see how they work."

Two hours later Momma called for us to come to the house. As she turned from the old cooking stove and saw me, she gasped "Oh, Christine, who cut your hair?" Ben had used the shears and cut my hair on one side of my head and not on the other side.

"Is it pretty, Momma?" I asked. "Ben found Grandpa's sheep shears."

"I did not, Momma," said Ben. "She fell off the porch"

Momma knew I didn't fall off the porch, but didn't punish Ben for his curiosity. I didn't think my mother liked my haircut though, because she did make it clear to Ben he was never to do that again.

That ended any chances Ben had of becoming a sheep shearer.

Without a mirror, I never knew how my hair looked after Ben cut it or after Momma cut it. The short hair made the hot temperatures more tolerable.

Shortly, after Maggie's fourth birthday, she received a haircut from Momma after Ben climbed a small tree and crawled out on a limb just above her. Maggie felt something hit her on the head. She continued to play, curious about the horrible odor.

Later, at the shack, Momma asked "Maggie, what is that smell?"

"I don't know Momma. I been smellin' it all day myself," replied Maggie.

"Come here Maggie," Momma said, reaching out her hand to pull Maggie toward her. Momma soon found the source of the odor and cut Maggie's hair to remove dried feces from it.

With our curiosity never exhausted, Maggie decided she would try her hand at cooking one day when Momma had to run an errand and left her in charge. Momma hardly ever left the place and we never asked any questions when she did.

"Look what I found!" Toby exclaimed after finding a bird's nest holding eggs.

"Well, I'll cook 'em," suggested Maggie, thinking the eggs would make a perfect meal. Maggie found the skillet and lard she needed in the kitchen. She set the skillet containing the lard on the hot cook stove and soon bird eggs were fried over easy, ready to eat.

Life on the mountain lacked boredom. We always enjoyed taking turns riding on top of the plow the horse pulled to plow the garden in the summer. Daddy told us it helped to hold the plow down. This seemed like fun to us.

When Daddy said I was big enough to stand on the plow, I didn't tell him I had to stand on my tiptoes to reach the clothesline.

One smoldering summer day a goat showed up on the property and a very hungry one, at that. It managed somehow to get in somebody's homemade moonshine still.

"Look at that ole goat!" laughed Jacob. We all started laughing, watching it stagger and shake its head.

"Why, that thang's crazy. You better not get too close!" warned Ben.

The next day, Momma hung some clothes on the line. When she returned later to get them, her very best dress had less material than it did when she hung it out.

"Momma, I bet that ole' goat ate it," I said.

I didn't see the goat any more until we went to a place we called the" Buzzard Cliff", a real scary place because it was so far down to the bottom. I wouldn't go and look over it without crawling on my belly. Ben's the only one who'd walk up to the edge. I was real scared he would fall. I crawled to the edge real careful like and looked over. I saw the ole goat laying at the bottom of the cliff. I never asked anybody what happened. I was afraid Momma wouldn't let me go back to the cliff.

CHAPTER FOURTEEN

Excitement on the Mountain!

The leaves being drained of the life in them and falling to earth let us know that winter was on its way. However, the absence of winter had offered potential for a good crop of black walnuts on the mountain. Me and Toby took advantage of winter's mercy late one evening.

Without a hammer, we used two rocks to crack the walnuts. We put the walnut on one rock and used the other rock to hit the walnut until it broke. We had to be careful or we'd hit our fingers. The temperature outside started dropping, but didn't interrupt our mission. After a while my hands started to ache like they were burning and then they turned blood red.

"I got some matches. Let's build a fire," suggested Toby.

"Are you sure we won't get in trouble?" I asked.

Toby, pulling the matches from his pocket, assured me, "It'll be alright."

Me and Toby gathered small dry sticks and soon had a fire going. A gust of wind carried some of the sparks to nearby dry leaves. The leaves were soon burning. Toby managed to put out the fire. As he turned, another gust of wind carried sparks to other dry leaves. Toby ran to put out that fire, but it started to spread quickly. His bare feet didn't hinder the fire and soon it laid claim on nearby sage grass.

While the blaze went higher into the air, Toby and I ran to the shack, scared half to death. "Momma, Momma!" yelled Toby.

Daddy heard Toby and saw the flames as did nearby neighbors. Neighbors ran toward the flames with rough burlap sacks, dull shovels and old quilts.

"Hurry up!" Daddy squalled.

They soon had the fire out, but not before it had done considerable damage to the timber.

I guess that's just about the most exciting thing we ever seen on the mountain.

Daddy told the men, who helped put out the fire, exactly what happened. Daddy said his honesty paid off when he didn't have to pay a big lot of money. I didn't know how much that was, but I didn't think we had it.

One afternoon Ben created a lot of excitement, too. It was different from the fire, but it sure shook us up!

"Where is Ben?" asked Momma, as we gathered around the table one afternoon.

"I don't know" replied Daddy.

"Do you young'uns' know anything?" asked Daddy, glancing from one of us to the other.

We sat silent for a few seconds. Finally, I spoke up. "Daddy, he left off the mountain early this mornin'."

"Where'd he go?" asked Daddy

"He said he wanted to visit Grandma," I informed Daddy.

"Patton, that's twenty miles away! Anything could happen to a nine year old boy!" Momma exclaimed.

Daddy stood up and stepped across the bench he was sitting on and walked briskly out the door.

"Oh, boy, Ben's gonna get it now!" said Toby "You shouldn't a told 'em'."

"No, he's not," I said. I was really afraid, but pretended not to be.

"You all dry up and finish eatin' or you're gonna get it!" Momma scolded us.

Momma got up from the table. Holding Sawyer, who had been sitting on her lap, she walked to the window and looked out. I watched Momma real close as she stood there and asked that man Jesus to bring Ben home safe.

Momma then returned to the table, making sure we all had something to eat.

After we ate, Maggie helped Momma change diapers and care for Jacob and Leon and I took my place on the straight back chair and began to wash dishes. Washing dishes became part of my daily chores before I reached the age of six. I hated it, especially the gravy skillet, but had to do it anyway. I don't know why Momma let the gravy skillet sit all day until I came home from school. That gravy was so dried on that old black cast iron skillet that I didn't think I'd ever get it off. I didn't understand why Ben and Luke couldn't wash dishes once in a while. I never did question it, though. I thought they had other chores to do.

Not long after Sawyer had fallen asleep, we heard a truck rattling up the driveway. Momma walked to the window and barely could see Mr. Honaker's truck with the sun hidden just over the mountain top. She watched as Daddy and Ben stepped out of the truck.

"He was at his grandma's." Daddy shook his head, walking slowly up the steps and into the house. Ben followed Daddy in the house. I was watching to see if he would get a whoopin'.

"Ben you had us all worried to death!" said Momma.

"I don't know how he walked that far, but he did," Daddy continued.

Momma responded "I don't know either, Patton, but I'm glad he's alright."

That was all I ever heard about the matter. I sure was glad Ben didn't get in trouble since I told on him.

CHAPTER FIFTEEN

June

Momma stood near the window holding Dean against her hip. "Big truc! Big truc!" he said over and over, pointing outside. He clapped his small hands together and then pointed again saying "Big truc!"

"Momma, I can't see. Make Leon get out of my way!" I complained, while balancing my weight on my tip toes and moving my head to one side.

"What is it?" asked Jacob.

Another question came from Ben,"Can I go out there, Momma?"

"No, you can't!" Momma promptly replied. "You all just need to calm down. You'll see her soon enough."

"See who? " Jacob asked, looking up at Momma.

"You will see June." Momma responded.

"Oh, Momma, are we gettin' another sister!?" I squealed with delight.

"Look!" said Momma, "There she is!"

Wide eyed, we watched a very healthy looking brown cow steadily step off the truck onto a rough wooden ramp leading into a dilapidated barn. The barn, held together with rusty nails driven into decaying sun bleached lumber, allowed the cow shelter without its tin roof falling on top of her.

"It's June!" I yelled" Not a sister, but a cow! Now we can have milk to drink!"

We could hardly contain our excitement as we watched the big truck go back down the driveway empty. We ran as fast as we could to the barn where Daddy and June stood.

"Stay back," warned Daddy "You might scare her."

One by one we all met June. She seemed to enjoy all the attention, getting' her head rubbed.

The next day early, I watched Daddy through the cracked upstairs window pane. He came from the barn carrying a bucket. I knew what the bucket contained. Anxiously, I ran down the creaky steps. "Milk, Daddy, we got milk!" I exclaimed.

We all enjoyed warm milk for breakfast that morning. June produced two peck-sized galvanized buckets of milk a day for us to drink and for cooking.

Churning the milk in a churn produced butter. However, it was a slow tedious process for the one doing the churning. Momma decided to ask Jacob to push the old churn up and down in the crock until the milk became thick. This could sometimes take hours.

Momma attended to other things and Jacob began to churn. Time passed quickly for Momma. She decided to see how the churning was going. She stepped out on the porch where she'd left Jacob with the churn. To her surprise, he had his little dirty feet holding the wooden lid on the churn as he pushed the paddle up and down. Momma relieved him of his duty and he came out to play with us.

Momma always remembered the incident and wondered just how much dirt fell from those little feet into the butter. Nonetheless, buttered cornbread was always a favorite part of our meal. She told Jacob, "Why, a little dirt never hurt nobody!" It could've been more than a little in that batch of butter!

Momma could often be seen carrying the empty galvanized bucket and walking toward the barn.

When the summer months began, bringing flies in abundance, June used her tail to swat the flies. This made milking the cow an unpleasant experience. Momma always asked one of us to hold the cow's tail until she finished milking the cow. We took turns, always wishing we could be playing with the others and not standing behind a cow, holding its tail.

One morning when it was Jacob's responsibility to hold the cow's tail, so it wouldn't swat Momma in the face, he stood quietly holding June's tail. He began to look around, bored like any youngster would be. He noticed a barbed wire fence directly behind him. His small mind devised a plan so he could come and play with us and June wouldn't swat Momma in the face with her tail. He pondered whether or not his plan would work.

Jacob grasped a small strand of the cow's tail and began to pull it back toward the fence. Wrappin' it around the wire he tied a hard knot in it securing it to the fence. Gently he pulled another strand and secured it to the fence, also. Since June didn't seem to mind, Jacob worked faster until he had her tail safely tied to the wire so she couldn't hit Momma with it. Jacob then slipped quietly away from June without Momma knowing what he had done.

June's anxiety seemed unusual to Momma, but Momma stayed calm and soon milk filled most of the bucket. Momma stepped back with the bucket and patted June on the hip, fully expecting the cow to move. June suddenly became hysterical! "Moooo!" the cow bellowed, followed by another loud "Mooooooo!"

Momma realized June's dilemma and tried to calm the cow, without results. Jacob heard Momma scream "Help!" as he peeked from around a tree up on the hill. He was too scared to go back to the barn.

The loud scream from Momma sent the cow bolting forward, leaving most of her tail behind hanging from the fence! It was an awful commotion and sight to behold!

Jacob, nearly as terrified as June, stayed away from the house all day, not willing to face Momma. He thought he was really in for a good switching. However, Momma decided Jacob had punished himself, going without food all day.

June's tail did heal in time. Maggie said Daddy had to sell her since he had no way of feeding her in the winter without grass. I cried as I watched June being forced back up the ramp and into a truck. I not only would miss the milk, but I'd become very attached to June. I often wondered what happened to her.

We found out later that Daddy had sold June to bond some man out of jail and he had to sell June to pay the bond. I don't know why Daddy did some of the things he did. I heard Momma say "He should've left the man in jail."

CHAPTER SIXTEEN

Where the Axe Falls, There Shall It Lay

We never knew what to expect from one day to the next. We didn't know what we we would eat, but we knew we'd always have something, if only a raw potato. However, that didn't stop us from being hungry most of the time. One day that hunger brought a lot of regret for me and Toby.

We were instructed to carry Daddy's lunch off the mountain to him. Daddy worked for the railroad at the time with a crew cutting props. I wasn't sure just what that meant, but that's what Momma said he was doing.

"Take this to your daddy. Be careful, don't drop it. You've seen him on your way to school and you know where he's at," Momma instructed us, giving us a brown paper bag holding a four pound lard bucket of cornbread and milk mixed together and a spoon. "Don't run." she told us.

Out of sight of the house and being hungry, Toby asked "Christine, do you think we could take just one bite? I'm hungry."

"We better not, Toby," I replied, while walking ahead of Toby, clutching the bucket tight, careful not to drop it.

"But, Christine, I'm hungry. I don't think Daddy would miss it. Besides, he don't know how much is in the bucket," pleaded Toby.

"Well, I guess you're right, Toby. He won't miss just a little bit of it." Toby and I used the clean spoon and ate some of Daddy's lunch. I knew we were doing something awful bad, but we were so hungry. I thought that man Jesus would understand and forgive us.

"We better not eat no more, Toby" My conscience was really bothering me after eating three spoons full.

"Okay, but it sure is good!" He spooned up one more bite then looked down at his bib overalls in search of a clean spot to wipe the spoon off. After rubbing the spoon across his bibs a couple of times, he carefully placed it back in the paper bag with the four pound lard bucket that contained what remained of Daddy's lunch.

I knew we needed to hurry and said to Toby "That's good enough, Toby. Momma said a little dirt never hurt nobody. We gotta go!"

We continued on, without saying a word. We finally got to the place where Daddy was working and gave him his lunch.

"Toby, let's don't tell nobody what we did. Then Momma and Daddy won't find out," I coached my younger brother as we walked up the mountain.

Toby quickly responded "Okay, Sis, I won't." We didn't have much else to say the rest of the way home. I figured Toby must have felt near as bad as I did.

Later, while we were all eating supper, Daddy asked, "Clarie, why didn't you send me more lunch than you did? It wasn't much for a working man."

Toby and I just looked at each other, fearful like.

Momma responded "Why Patton, it was almost full," and then stopped sudden as her eyes met with Daddy's. She watched him glance at us. They realized what happened. With nothing more said about the lunch, the subject quickly changed. I felt my face turning red and I didn't feel very hungry after that.

Daddy knew we'd been hungry, too. He delighted in knowing he had shared his lunch with us.

Toby and I always regretted eating Daddy's lunch. I didn't feel much like sleeping that night either. I asked that man Jesus to forgive me.

Some days on Black Top Mountain proved even more challenging than others. One day it became nearly unbearable for Maggie when she's only five years old. I knew that was how old Ben would be on his next birthday.

We had a special place to play some distance from the log shack. We called it the "Peach Tree Swag." We named a lot of the places where we played. Excited about playing there, Maggie, Ben and I ran all the way.

After arriving we found an ax stuck in a stump. We knew Blake had left it there, after chopping some wood. We didn't know where he had gone to.

Maggie decided she would chop some wood. After all, it seemed like the obvious thing to do, with no toys to play with. She grabbed the handle and pulled and pulled.

"Here, let me help ya'" said Ben. Together Maggie and Ben freed the ax.

As Ben stepped back out of the way, Maggie lifted the ax as far up as she could, but it proved to be too heavy for her to balance. Suddenly it hit the ground, leaving the end of her big toe laying nearby.

Maggie, crying something awful, picked up the end of her toe, and carried it home.

"Momma, Momma," Ben yelled when we could see the shack. "Come quick!"

Momma ran outside to see what happened. "Oh, dear God!" she hollered when she saw blood squirting from Maggie's toe. It was all dirty since she had to walk barefoot in the dirt. Maggie looked like she was going to fall over dead, but was still holding tight to the end of her toe. It scared me when I thought about Maggie dying.

Momma ran as fast as she could to get Uncle Lake. He carried Maggie off the mountain. She spent the night in a hospital. Daddy stayed with her and Uncle Lake buried the end of Maggie's toe.

Maggie's cries "Oh my toe!" echoed from tree top to tree top for many days while her foot healed.

Maggie later mashed the big toe on her other foot and kept saying she needed a doctor, but there was no doctor on the mountain for anybody to see. Momma wrapped it as best she could even though a lot of flesh hung from Maggie's toe. "Oh, my toe!" echoed again. I felt so sorry for Maggie, but there was nothing I could do to make it better. It did heal in time without her losing her other toe. I sure was glad because it about made me sick to look at it!

Awhile before Maggie had cut her toe off, Momma heard a splash one morning. It seemed like she just had a special way to know when something was wrong. She walked outside and there was Maggie in the big rain barrel! If Momma hadn't heard her, I guess she would've been gone that day. Momma said that man Jesus watched over us as if we were precious jewels, whatever that meant.

***

One morning, Momma was using two towels, holding one in each hand, to grasp a hot aluminum pan on each side. She carefully picked up the pan of hot water from atop the old cast iron cook stove. She slowly turned around, holding tight to the pan, and started walking toward a table where dirty dishes sat waiting to be washed. Momma didn't notice eight month old Patsy crawling in the direction she was walking with the pan of water. When Momma glanced down and saw Patsy, she stopped real fast, not wanting to step on Patsy.

Water suddenly splashed from the aluminum pan onto Patsy's naked little back. Before Momma could set the pan down, Patsy started screaming. Momma gently picked Patsy up as she continued to cry without stopping, holding her breath at times.

Momma yelled "Maggie, Maggie! Come here quick!"

A whole bunch of us came running to see what was wrong. One look at Patsy's back and I needed to ask no questions. Momma quickly handed Patsy to Maggie and grabbed some raw potatoes from a nearby bucket. Momma soon had them washed in cool water, sliced, scraped and laying on Patsy's back. Momma then laid a wet cloth on Patsy's little back over the potatoes.

Patsy began to calm down as Momma talked to her and began to talk to that man, Jesus.

Many more times Momma put raw potatoes on Patsy's back to draw the burn from her back, and her back did eventually heal. I was amazed by the way Momma knew exactly what to do no matter what happened to us.

Another time Leon had a boil on his arm. Momma went to the garden we had at the time and cut some tops off of some beets. She cooked them until they wilted and when they were cool enough, she put them on the boil. "Honey, you'll be alright now," Momma assured Leon. The next day the boil had disappeared.

One day while bathing Momma said she noticed a small knot under her chin. She said she ignored it thinking it'd go away. Its persistence not only kept it there, but it continued to grow. She said that she decided she'd act in faith and do something unusual. She'd heard somebody say that if she washed it with water from an old stump, it would go away.

Momma did find an old stump and approached it early one morning finding water in it. I went with her and she told me to wait at the edge of the woods until she came back. I could see her off in the distance. She threw the water on her neck where the knot was, refusing to allow any doubt to deter her. Within days, the knot began to go away.

Naomi Wood called the knot a "goiter." Momma was never bothered with it again.

Another time when Leon had thrush, momma did something strange. She sent me off the mountain to ask a neighbor to send her daughter to visit Momma. I hurried and came back with the neighbor's teenage daughter.

Momma asked the young girl to go breathe into Leon's mouth. She did as Momma asked and the next day Leon was free of the thrush.

Momma believed if a child that had never seen their daddy breathed into the mouth of somebody with the thrush, that person with the thrush would be healed. Momma said "All you need is faith like a grain of mustard seed."

I knew she had been talking to that man Jesus again.

CHAPTER SEVENTEEN

Determination and Desperation

Desperation became an ever present companion to Momma and us young'uns. Momma never gave up no matter how bad things may have seemed.

When the temperature began to drop in the log shack like any other winter evening, Momma knew it'd be even colder during the night. Knowing she lacked enough wood to last all night, she called for Ben and Luke. "I want you to go get some wood. I have to have it." She continued, "Bring me whatever you can find; anything."

My brothers put their coats on and stepped out into the cold. They returned a little later with broken planks of wood cradled in their arms. Momma didn't ask where the planks came from, elated to be able to keep us warm. The crackling of the fire in the pot belly stove sounded like music to us.

As the evening sun hid its glory, Daddy returned home and nearly fell as he stepped onto the porch.

Later, at the table, while reaching for a piece of cornbread, Daddy inquired, "Clarie, what happened to the boards on the front porch floor?"

Momma coughed trying not to choke on the food in her mouth, unable to speak. She looked at Ben sitting directly across the table from her. While Ben's gaze focused on Luke, both boys remained silent.

Momma regained her composure, answering her husband, "We needed wood Patton, and I told the boys to bring me some. A front porch ain't no good if my children freeze to death."

Daddy said "That's the truth, Clarie. Do what you have to do."

"Poor people's got poor ways," Momma concluded.

The porch floor became smaller as the old shack became warmer. Momma considered it a good trade off, though everybody had to be especially careful so as not to fall on the naked ground the boards once covered.

We were not old enough to chop down trees. I was only seven years old at the time. We couldn't find enough wood under the snow during the winter months to keep two fires going. We carried buckets and burlap sacks of coal up the steep mountainside at times to supplement the wood. We scooped up what coal we could get from where a tipper had been at a nearby mine. We never thought of it as stealing, but kind of like eating the crumbs that fall from a table.

The coal felt real heavy and it was hard to carry. Sometimes we had to stop because it hurt our shoulders so bad, but it seemed worth it to us so we could stay warm. Of course we didn't know anything about freezing to death, but heard Momma tell Daddy she didn't want us to. We didn't want to, either.

Many winter mornings, we awoke to a white blanket of snow covering our bed as well as the mountains around us. I didn't get as excited as my brothers did about the snow.

"It snowed!" said Luke as he jumped out of bed.

"Oh boy!" yelled Sawyer.

Once Luke and Sawyer appeared in the kitchen, Momma knew exactly what they wanted. "It's over there," she said, pointing to a round large aluminum pan sometimes used to hold dirty dishes.

"Make sure it's clean." Momma reminded them.

It didn't take my brothers but a short time to fill the large pan with the cleanest, whitest snow they could find.

Later that afternoon, we received a generous portion of homemade snow ice cream. Momma added milk and vanilla flavoring to the snow and let it refreeze to create the special treat. Sometimes she added chocolate if she had it. That was my favorite, but it didn't happen often.

Momma made lye soap from cooking the intestines of a hog so we could be clean. "It's ok to wear rags, as long as they're clean rags" she told us, after a day of ridicule at school. If it was warm enough my brothers wore bibs with no shirt underneath. Sometimes the pant legs were rolled up if they were too long.

We were barefoot most of the time. Walking up and down the mountain quickly wore out a pair of shoes. Aunt Nan bought me a beautiful pair of black shoes one time. I was so excited to have new shoes. They were falling off my feet in less than a week!

The trees had been cleared to provide a road up the mountain to the shack, but Daddy didn't own a car. A horse and buggy provided transportation in times past. Not much more than a wide trail, our footsteps kept grass from growing on it.

The only socks we had were given to us from someone who already wore them until they had holes in them. If my brothers were given any blue jeans, they'd have holes worn in the knees. I guess people felt sorry for us and didn't throw anything away. We were always glad to get clothes even if they did have holes in them.

One evening Momma noticed Jacob scratching his head a lot.

"Come here, Jacob, let me look at your head," Momma told him. Jacob stood beside Momma. She carefully parted his hair and looked at his scalp. "Yea, just what I thought; head lice," said Momma.

Though it created a lot of extra work for Momma, she used lye soap to rid us of the lice, telling us "It's not a disgrace to get head lice, but it is to keep them." I sure didn't want them again, because Momma scrubbed my head until it hurt.

Our living conditions made my family susceptible to many different things, such as worms, colds, bed bugs, viruses, whooping cough, chicken Pox, and measles. It seemed Momma always had something unpleasant to deal with. I thought that was why nobody wanted to sit beside us at school.

One time when we all got a cold, Daddy went to the mountains and dug sassafras roots. Momma boiled them and made tea for us to drink. It did make me feel better. Sometimes she fried an onion and laid it on my chest and my fever broke. She said that man Jesus showed her what to do.

Having chores to do before school, walking off the mountain to go to school and having little to eat made it very difficult for us to concentrate on our school work. Being bullied along with everything else made it nearly impossible.

I remember one day at school when someone gave me a small apple pie. It's the only time I remember anyone giving me anything. I was so hungry and it looked so good, but I thought about all my little brothers having so little to eat most of the time. Even though I didn't have anything to eat that morning, I couldn't eat it knowing my little brothers were hungry.

I carried the pie all afternoon and all the way back up the mountain. When the shack came into view I saw three year old Dean playing in the dirt.

"Dean, come here, I got somethin' for ya'!" I hollered when I got closer to the shack.

He came running as fast as his short little legs would carry him.

"What is it?" He eagerly wanted to know.

I gave him the pie and watched him eat it and lick his dirty little hands. Tears came to my eyes as I thought about how much it meant to him.

"Thank you, Christine," Dean said before he went running back to his imaginary playground.

I felt good that my little brother got something special to eat. I learned that day that it really is better to give than receive. I never forgot the lesson I learned that day.

CHAPTER EIGHTEEN

Ten Little Toes

Long before daddy sold June, the four oldest of us young'uns had to take turns going out to the barn in the morning before school to get the cow up and milk her. When the cow stood up, we placed our cold feet on the warm hay. We also learned that the cow urine healed our feet if we had cuts or sores on them.

In the Spring, dust blew around our feet as Maggie and I swept the bare yard with two old straw brooms. We knew it was getting warm enough to play outside and Momma didn't want us to cut our bare feet. The warm weather was so delightful!

We never knew in advance what a summer day had reserved for us.

A salt block, placed near the barn for the cattle, appeared very beneficial to us one day. The cattle were licking the salt when we decided we needed salt for the green apples we were eating. The large cattle were no match for eight little dirty feet running toward them as fast as we could move. Afraid of the strange sight, the cattle left the salt block for us to enjoy. They walked some distance away and turned to watch us rub our apples across the salt block before we took a bite.

While Momma didn't run the neighbor's cattle away from their salt block, she did insist they share the fruit of the field with her. Momma had learned early in life which plants are edible and which ones are not. We loved wandering about looking for something Momma could cook.

"Can we eat this, Momma?" asked Toby, running toward Momma.

"How 'bout this one, and this one?" asked Ben as he clutched the Dandelion and Briar Tops.

Momma unfolded the small hand and remarked "Yes, Ben, I can cook that. Bring me more like it." She then turned her attention to Toby as he held up Lambs Quarter and Burdock to get

Momma's approval. My small hand held edible plants, too, she said.

Momma's heart filled with pride as she watched us gather the plants she showed us. Later that evening we sat around the table, enjoying the mixture of cooked edible plants we'd helped gather.

"Can we get some more tomorrow?" asked Jacob, while chewing his food.

"We will see," said Momma, hoping she could find time to supervise the small crew to keep us away from poisonous plants.

Our eagerness to look for food reflected our hunger. Unfortunately, Momma couldn't always protect us.

"Momma, Momma!" I yelled as I burst through the front door. "Jacob is sick! He's gonna die! He ate some of that bad stuff you told us to leave alone!"

Momma ran to Jacob as fast as she could, knowing from experience how sick eating the wrong plant can make a person.

"Jacob, what did you eat!?" Momma asked.

Maggie held up what Momma had called mold weed. "This is it, Momma. Me and Toby ate it, too. Are we gonna die?" Maggie started to cry.

"Go get some lard and be quick about it!" Momma instructed Luke and I. We did as we were told.

The others followed us into the kitchen. I could hear Leon crying in the distance, but Momma couldn't worry about him right now. I was hoping she wouldn't tell me to pick him up, because I was worried about Maggie and Jacob.

Momma heated the lard until it melted. While holding Jacob on her lap, she forced him to drink some of the warm lard. He began to vomit. "Oh, Momma, I don't wanna die." Jacob said holding his stomach and crying.

"You'll be sick awhile, but you won't die." Momma assured him, as he continued to rid his digestive system of the poison. "Christine, check on the little ones." Momma said, while giving Maggie and Toby some of the lard.

It seemed Momma always knew what to do and the three did recover after a hard lesson about poisonous pants.

Poke salad, a favorite of Momma's, grew larger in size and we could easily recognize it. Momma cooked a raccoon or a groundhog if the neighbors gave her one. We were glad to get anything to eat.

CHAPTER NINETEEN

Food on the Table!

"Today is the day!" announced Maggie, throwing the covers back.

"Yes!" I responded while slipping my feet into my flip-flops.

In the next room, we could hear the boys talking while they dressed. "I wonder what it'll be this time." Jacob said.

Luke replied "I don't really care. I just know it'll be good!" Soon we were all down stairs, unable to hide our excitement, ready to walk down off the mountain, heading to school.

All day we could hardly concentrate on our lessons. It seemed as if the school day would never end. My stomach kept growling loud and sometimes the teacher gave me a weird look.

Finally, at the end of the day we stepped off the big yellow bus. We were at the foot of the mountain, but this time we didn't go straight home. Daddy was waiting for us at the nearby store. We saw Daddy sitting on the familiar rock wall with brown bags and small boxes sitting on the gravel near his feet. We ran and began to pick up the bags and boxes. Maggie and Ben carried the heaviest ones, but we all wanted to carry something.

I carried a small box and hurried up one of the paths leading to the log shack. Suddenly I heard a flutter and jumped, nearly dropping the box I carried. A quail came running toward me with its feathers ruffled. I thought it to be a momma protecting her babies.

I sat the box down and watched as the quail went back to its nest. I continued to watch for a few minutes, but it never returned. I then picked up my box and started back up the road. I never saw the quail again.

Standing near the window, with a big smile on her face, Momma watched us come up the road carrying the brown bags and boxes. Though not sure what the boxes and bags held, she knew it would be more than we had.

She met us at the door and helped us set the bags and boxes on the long table. We began to pull boxes of powdered milk and powdered eggs from the bags, along with other groceries. It was a rare occasion to have this much food on the table at one time.

"What's in this box?" Jacob asked excitedly, as he held a box up with both hands.

"Be careful, you'll drop it," warned Momma.

"Oh, wow, we got cheese!" Maggie yelled, lifting up the five pound roll. "Can we have some on biscuits, Momma? I'm hungry."

When the government gave out food once a month to qualifying families, it made the day very special for hungry young'uns'. Momma baked biscuits so we could eat cheese biscuits. We slept that night without hunger pains interrupting our rest, but the groceries didn't last very long with so many to feed.

I not only had to wash dishes each day, but I also had to make cornbread. I became very bored with that responsibility. I decided I'd find a way to ruin it and then I wouldn't have to make it each day.

I looked around and saw something on a shelf. I'd heard Momma call it baking powder, so it seemed good to use. Barely able to reach it and nearly falling off the chair, I did manage to get it off the shelf. With my small hand I turned it up and sprinkled some into the cornbread mix. "That should do it," I said aloud. I managed to put the box back on the shelf without cracking my head open on the wooden floor.

Later, while we sat around the table, I watched Momma take a bite of the cornbread. I swung my feet back and forth under the table, wondering if l would get in trouble. I thought it would be worth it as long as I didn't have to make cornbread again.

Momma, looking directly at me, asked "Christine, what'd you do to this cornbread?" Then she blurted out, "Why, it's the best I ever eat!"

I was so surprised I nearly fell off the bench!

"It's really good, "remarked Daddy, taking another bite and then scooping up some brown beans with a spoon.

I decided since my plan fell through, I'd pretend to be a great cook. "Oh, I just added a little bakin' powder," I said proudly.

Daddy replied "Well, we know who'll make the cornbread around here from now on!"

Momma sometimes made cornbread gravy or what we called "mush." When she did that I got a break from making the cornbread.

Momma also taught me how to mix canned milk, water and Karo syrup to make formula for the babies.

We picked berries when in season and sold them to buy canned milk at the store for the babies. We'd get fifty cents a gallon for them. Sometimes we found enough for Momma to can some in a half gallon jar. When winter came, she opened them and made dumplin's. We poured milk over them. They were delicious!

Aunt Lectie, as we called her, showed us kindness. They had only two children to feed and fiared much better than we did. She gave us buttermilk and milk when she had it to spare. One day she gave us a burlap sack full of apples. Toby and I borrowed the Yancey's mule and rode her bareback to go get the apples.

When we got to Uncle Ralph's house, he threw the sack of apples across the mule's back between Toby and I. We got about half way home and the apples slid off into the road. We got off the mule and found out just how long its legs were! Toby tried and tried to lift the apples back up on his back. I was very little help in the conquest. We thought that ole mule had the longest legs we had ever seen on an animal!

After many failed attempts, Toby said "Christine, I got an idea. Let's drag the apples on the side of the bank and move the mule over there and then we'll both sling the apples up on it."

So we both drug the apples to the side of the road and up the bank. We moved the gentle mule and she just stood there waiting for further directions.

Toby grabbed one side of the sack and I grabbed the other and away went those apples right up on that mule's back! We managed to get back on the mule and finally made it home with the apples. I don't know when apples ever tasted so good! We told Momma what happened. She said "You done good." I don't recall Aunt Lectie giving us any more apples after that.

It was music to our ears to hear "pop, pop.....pop" while Momma shook the old skillet on top of the wood stove with one hand and held a lid on it with the other. Soon we were all sitting on the floor and eating popcorn—a very special treat.

I sat down at the long wooden table to eat my supper one evening, expecting the usual brown beans and cornbread. However, a huge boiled hog's head sit right in the middle of the table!

"That looks like a hog's head!" said Toby. Leon and Sawyer began to laugh at the strange sight.

Sawyer spoke up "Why that thang's lookin' right at us!"

Sure enough, that cooked hog still had its eyes in its head!

Daddy said" Yall need to stop laughin' and be thankful for anything you got to eat." Then he thanked that man Jesus for our food.

We all had some meat with our bread that night and we slept sound as a result. That hog's head was something someone else was going to throw away, but Momma was glad to get it for us to eat. We'd take anything nobody else wanted.

Patton and Clara Compton with eleven children. Clara was pregnant with Patsy at the time the picture was taken. It was taken in the early spring, 1958, just before leaving the mountain.

PART 2: THE PROMISED LAND

CHAPTER TWENTY

Makin' Plans

After Momma's brother, Uncle Henry, became another statistic in a mining accident Momma vowed none of her eight sons would work in the coal mines.

I overheard Momma talking to Daddy. "Patton, I wanna move off the mountain."

Agreeing with Momma, Daddy said "Clarie, I'll see what I can do."

"Patton, I know there's a way to get my children to a better place," Momma continued.

I didn't tell anyone but Luke what I heard Momma and Daddy talking about.

"Luke, I think we're goin' to the promise land Momma's been singin' about!" Luke was almost as excited as I was!

"Really, Christine? How do you know? When are we leavin'?"

"I don't know everthing about it, but I did hear 'em," I told him.

We didn't mention it to anyone else, even though the thought kept me awake the same night. I wondered what life would be like in the Promised Land. I'd heard my teachers talking about pioneers going to a new land, so I believed Daddy would take us to a new land. Would we be like the pioneers? Would we have to build a cabin? Would it be far away? Was it a real pretty place like the heaven Daddy had told us about?

Looking out the window, into the moonlight, my mind drifted back in time remembering life on Black Top Mountain:

Like any other youngster his age, Luke didn't lack enthusiasm when it came to a new toy, especially when it resulted from his imagination.

A long slender piece of rubber held much potential for a seven year old boy. He thought of endless possibilities of how he could use the piece of rubber he found. An opportunity like this would only come once in his life time, he reasoned.

Luke looked for a stick. However, not just any old stick would do. It had to be forked. His excitement grew when, after searching relentlessly, he spotted the perfect stick. He worked feverously until he attached the rubber securely to the stick, thus yielding a slingshot. Finding rocks took little effort and soon the he hurled rock after rock through the air with his homemade slingshot. He pulled back on the rubber sling with great pride. He tried to hit birds and nearly took a squirrel off a limb. He wanted some squirrel gravy for dinner.

He heard the chickens cackling near the chicken coop and decided he'd test his skills on Sunday dinner. He pulled back as far as he could on the rubber sling while holding the rock tight. All at once he released it in the directions of the chickens. The rock flew through the air, causing the fearful chickens to scatter. Luke heard a thump and knew he'd hit something.

"Oh, boy, I got 'im!'" Luke exclaimed, jumping up in the air and waving his arms.

As Luke drew close to the chicken coop he could see something red just inside the door. His excitement grew. He got closer and ran as fast as he could toward the coop, realizing his target had not been a chicken at all. He raced toward me as I lay on the floor of the coop! Blood ran down the side of my head.

Luke hadn't noticed me sitting in the doorway of the coop. He quickly helped me into the shack, and watched while Momma bandaged my head with some old rags. Momma then found enough warm water to relieve me of the chicken droppings attached to me.

A few days later I felt as though nothing happened to me. Momma later told Luke, "Christine is the funniest lookin' chicken I ever saw!"

Luke still enjoyed his slingshot. As hard as he tried he couldn't make any contributions toward Sunday dinner. It really frustrated him how often squirrels could be seen in the tree tops unafraid.

Wild grapes became part of my memories as I lay awake in bed.

Luke and I, on our usual quest of curiosity, found a very large grape vine with wild grapes hanging in clusters. The grapes too high to reach, we decided to go home and get Daddy's crosscut saw.

"I'm tired," I said, trying to catch my breath.

"That's all right," said Luke   .

We carried the saw back to the location of the grapevine. With me on one end and Luke on the other end of the long rusty crosscut saw, we worked persistently.

Stopping to rest, I stated "I'm not sure I can do this, Luke."

"We're almost done now. Let's get back to work," he encouraged me. "We can do it."

Once more we began sawing. Soon the grapevine surrendered and came falling down. We looked up just in time to see it stop on a big tree limb. "Oh, no!" Luke and I said in unison. Luke began to pull on the vine, with little results.

"I got an idea," I exclaimed, "We'll climb up there and get 'em!"

Luke agreed and so we started carefully making our way up the vine. We found all the grapes we cared to eat. We thought about our siblings, picking all we could manage to carry home in Luke's shirt.

Momma thanked that man Jesus for our safety.

Our courageous efforts paid off when Momma made jam for the whole family to enjoy.

At one end of the yard, a log about four feet long served as a chopping block to split wood. This log held fascination for us all. Two holes leading underneath the log seemed a perfect place to play. I pretended the two holes led into coal mines. I found old corn cobs and pushed into the holes after putting rocks in them.

The rocks became trucks in my mind and I pushed them, one at a time, into the hole and thought I felt something cold against my hand. It seemed I could feel something cold moving, but thought it was only one of the rocks I'd pushed into the damp area. I continued to play, moving my "trucks" in and out of the "coal mines" while down on my knees. Soon I put my entire weight on the ground leaning against the log. I made a sound like that of a diesel truck as I moved one "truck" after another in and out of the pretend mines.

Again I felt something cold under the log. However, this time it appeared to be soft, not hard like a rock. When Maggie appeared a few minutes later, I told her about feeling something unusual under the log. Maggie decided to go back into the shack and tell Momma about the strange happenings. With Daddy gone at the time, Momma felt grateful a neighbor stopped by for a visit. She asked the gentleman visitor if he'd find out what lay under the log. The neighbor, Mr. Underwood approached me with a hoe in his hand.

Off in the distance Daddy could be seen walking toward the house. Increasing his speed, he soon stood near the log. Mr. Underwood stood beside the log and pushed the hoe against it to roll it over. As the log rolled over, he cautioned me and Maggie to step back away from it. We stood back at a distance. To everyone's amazement, two black copperheads appeared! As they tried to slither away, they couldn't escape the sharp edge of the garden hoe in Mr. Underwood's hand!

The "coal mine" never reopened, but the log still served as a chopping block. However, it was checked for snakes first.

The mountains contained a variety of snakes, some poisonous and others not. I drifted off to sleep that night while thinking about another close call I had.

It happened one morning when heavy dew blanketed the ground. With it not being a school day, I went outside early to play. Running and skipping, I played near a blackberry patch. I must've got too close to the claimed territory of a black racer snake, because when I turned to go in another direction, there he stood on his tail! He only had about six inches of his lower body on the ground and the rest was straight in the air! With his tongue sticking out, he leaned toward me.

I turned and ran as fast as my legs would carry me! I never did look back! I collapsed just inside the door of the shack, shaking with fright.

I decided to let the snake eat the blackberries from then on.

CHAPTER TWENTY ONE

The Exodus

Daddy sold the shack and the land for one thousand and seven hundred dollars. Two bay horses were included in the deal in addition to the money.

Our last night on the mountain we slept on feather mattresses on the floor with coats over us to keep us warm. Everything else filled the beds of two trucks sitting outside the shack.

We were anxious to leave and go to the Promised Land. Thoughts of what it would be like kept me awake.

I was nearing my fourteenth birthday and understood a whole lot of things better than I had before. I felt real good about leaving the mountain. I understood that shadow that taunted Momma for so long was not really a shadow, but an evil presence. I felt that at times, too, but didn't understand why it tried to make me feel so bad. I knew that man Jesus helped my family all those years and I wanted His help, too.

I got on my knees on the bare mattress the night before we left. I asked that man Jesus for a better life. Just like my mother, I wanted my own family. I asked Him to put somebody special in my life. I told Him I was sorry for eating Daddy's lunch and for everything I did that was bad. I started to cry as I talked to Him. I told Him I didn't understand everything, but knew He could help me. I knew I got awful carsick before, when Daddy took me to Grundy to have a tooth pulled, and I was real scared about going to the Promised Land. I asked Him to help me not to get sick. When I got up off my knees that night, I felt different. It was like I was all clean. I felt happy about where we were going. I knew everything would be alright. I felt I knew that man Jesus and He was my friend.

My family, with the help of neighbors, moved away from Black Top Mountain on April 2, 1960. Maggie stayed behind with one of the neighbors to finish out the school year. Little did we know that the last night spent on Black Top Mountain would be the last night all of Momma's children would sleep under the same roof.

Daddy managed somehow to get the trucks close to the shack. One of the trucks pulled a trailer transporting the two bay horses.

A neighbor drove his station wagon. Momma and three of us sat on the front seat of the station wagon and five young'uns sat on the back seat. Snow swirling in the cold air, settling in large piles, hindered our way to the vehicles. With excitement, determination and cold, wet feet, I climbed into the back seat of that old station wagon, wondering how we'd ever get off the mountain in it.

The trees that were like bars holding us captive bowed in the wind as we started down the driveway. It was as if they surrendered to the rattle of an old station wagon and two trucks taking us to the Promised Land. Momma never looked back when the vehicles started down the steep terrain.

I was afraid maybe something would happen and we'd have to turn around. I silently kept praying for a safe trip.

Uncle Lake and his grown son, Harry, also moved to Craig County with us. It seemed to me they had nowhere else to go. Uncle Lake stopped in Richlands and got him a pint of Peach Brandy. I never saw him drink Brandy before that day. I guess he was celebrating.

Luke and Toby filled a vacancy on the back of one truck in between two mattresses, since we couldn't all fit in the station wagon. I kept thinking about how cold they must've been.

Luke, excited about going to the Promised Land, raised his head to see where we were at.

"Are we there yet?" Luke asked.

Before Toby could answer, a limb hit the twelve year old on the side of his head. Luke sat back down between the mattresses. Toby noticed Luke had a real bad cut on his head.

Toby began to beat on the cab of the truck trying to get the attention of the neighbor driving the truck. Unable to get his attention, he broke a spindle out of one of the old ladder back chairs and beat on the cab of the truck with it.

The driver finally pulled the truck over to the side of the road. It was obvious we'd have to stop at the nearest clinic to have stitches put in Luke's head. Luke didn't realize we hadn't even got off the mountain yet.

While the three vehicles sat in the parking lot of the clinic, Daddy went inside with Luke. When the doctor walked in, Luke quickly informed him as to what was going on. "We're goin' to the Promised Land!" he exclaimed. He remembered hearing Momma sing *"I am bound for the Promised Land."*

It took nine stitches to sew up the cut on Luke's head. After that Luke and Daddy walked back outside to the parking lot.

The cackling chickens began to lay eggs in the back of the truck. Ben and I tried to catch the eggs before they hit the ground, excited at the thought of eggs for breakfast! Toby and Sawyer then started to help us. We never saw so many eggs!

"I got it!" Toby yelled.

"I got one, too!" Sawyer responded.

A woman inside the clinic kept coming to the window and looking out. I wondered if she had ever saw a chicken before.

"Clarie, can you find somethin' to put these eggs in?" Daddy asked.

Momma later said she didn't see how those chickens laid all those eggs. She said the rooster must've laid some, too! I concluded the chickens to be as excited as us about going to the Promised Land.

Ben, Luke and Toby sat all squished up together in the cab of one of the trucks the rest of the trip, so there wouldn't be any more mishaps with tree limbs.

Since Daddy made the arrangements for us to move, he'd already seen the house. However, Momma had not.

"Are we ever gonna get there?" asked Sawyer, squirming around on the back seat of the station wagon.

"Sawyer, scoot over, you got all the seat"
Leon complained, with his arms folded in front of
him.

"I do not!" replied Sawyer.

Reggie, who sat on my lap, began to cry.
Libby told her little brother "You'll be all right," as
she rubbed his arm. Patsy slept in Momma's arms.
Momma wondered how she could sleep through so
much commotion. Soon Reggie fell asleep.

With ten people riding in the station wagon, it
didn't take many miles until it became a very
uncomfortable ride. We went through four counties
that day before arriving at our new home nearly
four hours after leaving Black Top Mountain. We
moved from southwest Virginia to Craig County.

Our amazement became evident as we began
to ask questions. "Are we moving in that house?"
Leon asked, pointing to a beautiful white two story
house with a big yard and fence.

"No, Leon," I said.

"Are we gonna have a farm, Momma?" asked Jacob, gazing at cattle eating hay near a barn beside the road.

Sawyer quickly spoke up "I ain't workin' on no farm. But I do wanna horse."

Momma interrupted our chatter,"Young'uns, dry up or you'll wake up Patsy and Reggie."

We tried to honor Momma's wishes, but every once in a while Momma heard one of us say "Look at that!" or "Ain't that somethin'?" She knew we were taking a trip for the first time and seeing a lot we'd never even dreamed of ever seeing. The nice houses could hardly be comprehended in our young minds after being raised in a four room shack.

"Momma, can we stop at a store? I'm thirsty," asked Jacob, stretching his arms up over his head and yawning.

Patsy woke up and began crying. Dean started asking for something to eat. Momma had nothing to give us to eat or drink; only a bottle for Patsy.

"We'll be at the house soon." said Momma.

I wondered what our new home in the Promised Land would be like. Daddy made it sound very nice. It had to be better than what we left behind. Momma knew we'd have a better life away from the mountain, but I don't think any of us expected what lay ahead.

The driver, following the two trucks, stopped the car in front of a store. The store was a welcome sight, even though it could've used a coat of paint.

"Why are we stoppin'?" Leon asked.

"Be still and sit in the car unless you gotta use the johnny house." Momma told us.

"I gotta go," Sawyer said.

"Me, too," Dean spoke up.

We took turns wading through the snow making our way to the johnny house behind the store.

Back in the car, Momma handed us all something wrapped up in some kind of paper I never saw before.

"What is this thang?" asked Leon.

"It's a hot dog," Momma replied, "Eat it and hush."

"Don't look like no dog to me," Sawyer blurted out, just before taking a bite. "But it tastes good!" he continued.

"Stop talkin' with your mouth full!" Momma scolded him.

Libby looked at the hot dog Momma was eating. "Dog? That's a dog?" she asked. She took a bite of the hot dog in Momma's hand.

The boys in the back seat started giggling.

"This sure is fancy," said Sawyer, holding up a paper napkin. The boys started to giggle again.

"Finish eatin', we have to get goin'." Momma wiped her mouth with a paper napkin. I watched Momma fold the napkin and put it in her pocket.

I ate two hot dogs that day, finding the strange food to be the best I ever ate.

In less than an hour after stopping, we were back on the road.

Big farms and nice homes adorned the landscape on each side of the road. We were mesmerized by it all. It seemed like a dream.

Our excitement faded as hours of being cramped up in the backseat of a car seemed to lengthen.

The sound of the driver's voice startled me. "There it is!"

"Oh, my!" gasped Momma.

"Look at that!" I exclaimed, wide-eyed.

Toby questioned, "Are you sure this is it?"

A small creek with frozen edges winded its way through the property and a small narrow bridge provided a way across it. Snow drifts dominated the narrow driveway, keeping the vehicles at a distance. Armed with shovels, the men attempted to conquer the persistent layers of snow. Large gusts of wind hampered their efforts.

"Let's hook the horses to a truck and see if we can get closer to the house," suggested Daddy. The horses marched through the snow effortlessly, pulling the trucks behind them.

Not long afterwards, our meager possessions lay atop the white blanket of snow. The drivers took the trucks and the station wagon back to the mountains of southwest Virginia.

Two chimneys jutted from the roof of the two story house, hugged by a large porch. A large swing beckoned, in spite of snow covering it. Tall trees graced the property.

Stepping over the threshold, I immediately noticed the beautifu hardwood floor under my wet, numb feet. A real floor that I couldn't wait to sweep!

I ambled from room to room, stopping to look at walls without cracks in them and glass window panes. I thought this surely had to be the Promised Land.

"I want this room!" I heard a voice I barely recognized as my own. I'd never had an option about where to sleep and deciding proved to be a difficult task. I was afraid I'd wake up and be back on the mountain.

Momma, holding Patsy, walked inside and immediately noticed a bare light bulb in the ceiling.

"We have juice," Momma said, pulling a string attached to the fixture holding a naked bulb. The room lit up. When I saw the flash, I hurried outside to tell the others.

"Juice! Real juice!" said Toby, bolting through the door.

An abundant spring flowed freely just behind the house, offering' easy access to water.

"Come here young'uns and help carry this stuff!" Daddy yelled.

Since we were hesitant to leave the grandeur of the new home, Daddy found it necessary to call a second time.

"Come on. You can see all that later. We gotta get this stuff across the creek before dark." The seriousness in his tone let us know we better listen.

Once outside, we realized our belongins' had to be carried up a hill and across the narrow bridge before they could occupy the house.

"I didn't know we owned this much stuff," remarked Luke.

"Where'd it all come from, anyhow?" asked Toby.

"I don't have no idea." Luke's voice reflected his impatience.

Exhausted and excited at the same time, we were all soon wrapped up in our coats fast asleep on mattresses scattered around on the cold floor.

I knew we were free from the icy grip of Black Top Mountain. I closed my eyes and thanked Jesus for answering my prayer, knowing He'd went out of His way to do more than I had asked of Him. The Promised Land sure was something!

And I didn't get sick the entire way.

CHAPTER TWENTY TWO

New Challenges

The next morning, I opened my eyes and stared at the ceiling. I stood up, feeling a strange way I'd never felt before. Was this really the way people around here lived? The crackling of a fire delighted my ears and I was drawn to the warmth radiating from a wood stove.

I walked outside on the big porch. The bare tree tops yielded to the strong wind gusts. Nevertheless, illuminating rays of sunshine found their way through. I pulled my coat tighter around me, attempting to discourage the wind.

"Come in here Christine, and help make the gravy and fry these eggs," I heard Momma holler.

I knew I had to help Momma take care of Reggie and Patsy and my curiosity would have to wait to be satisfied.

I guess the floor was not level where Daddy set the bench behind the table, because it went backwards while the boys were eating breakfast. They were all okay, but I remember Momma hollering "Somebody get little Sawyer!" Somehow he ended up underneath the table while everyone else sitting on the bench went backward. I think Momma thought he was dead. I really thought it to be funny when I saw that nobody got hurt. Daddy made sure it didn't happen again.

With breakfast over, it came time to get everything in order. The boys carried beds and boxes upstairs. I helped unpack what few belongings we had.

Later that same day, some of us young'uns' went barefoot into the creek to catch the strange things swimming around. Daddy called them fish. We never saw any before, but Momma said she could cook them.

Blankets of white stretched out on the banks of the creek. The ice at its edges disclosed the chill of the water. Not deterred, we armed ourselves with burlap sacks, refusing to go home empty-handed. One of the neighbors called us "wild Indians." I didn't know exactly what they meant by that. I never had seen a wild Indian, though they talked about them at school.

Momma fried the fish in a cast iron skillet, but they were full of small bones, so we didn't bother to catch any more.

I didn't know chicken could be fried until we moved off the mountain and had more chicken to eat. Momma always fixed chicken and dumplin's back on the mountain so it'd go further. The fried chicken disappeared fast after it was put on the table. I was lucky to get a wing.

We were amazed by the rolling hills and the farm land and not having to walk up and down the mountain. Walking remained our main source of transportation, but we could wear a pair of shoes longer than a week before they fell off our feet.

Nearby neighbors owned a huge farm with cattle dotting the hillsides. Included in their livestock was a bull. We'd never saw a bull before and never saw so many cows in one place.

The neighbor's bull let out an extremely loud bellowing sound as it threw its head up in the air.

Dean stood nearby it with a fence between them. Never hearing a bull before, it frightened him. Knowing Daddy walked to the store just over the next hill and used the neighbor's field as a shortcut, Dean feared the worst. He yelled as loud as he could, "That ole bull's done went and killed Daddy!"

Most of us heard Dean yell and ran in his direction.

Toby immediately spoke up "We'll go kill that ole bull! He won't hurt nobody else."

One by one, we grabbed anything we could find. One picked up the broom from off the front porch; another grabbed a long stick that was laying in the yard. Toby ran to the chopping block and grabbed the ax. Luke saw a hoe leaned against the house.

"Come on. I'm ready!" Luke exclaimed.

Ben managed to get a pitch fork out of a nearby building and handed me a shovel he found. We was not sure how Daddy had accumulated so many tools, but we were sure thankful that day.

Momma was inside the house taking care of Patsy, Reggie and Libby, and didn't hear all the racket.

Eight of us crying, upset that Daddy was gone and determined to kill the neighbor's bull, started walking in the direction of the bull. We didn't know what we were going to find.

Jacob said, "We'll teach that ole bull." He shook the stick he held up in the air and used his other hand to wipe his nose.

"I'll poke his eyes out!" Leon added, gripping the stick he held a little tighter.

We came to the gate and opened it and walked into the field with the bull. I tried to act brave, but I was scared. I thought somebody else might get killed.

The bull just stood there looking at us. I don't think we intimidated him at all.

Suddenly, we heard somebody holler. "What in the world are yall doin'?"

We turned and saw Daddy coming over the top of the hill. He stopped, having no idea why we were coming toward him with an ax, shovel, pitch fork and a garden hoe, not to mention big sticks.

We dropped whatever we held and ran toward Daddy. We were so glad to see him. I was especially glad, because I really didn't think we could kill that bull without a gun of some kind. I was afraid we would just make him mad. I never did tell the others how I felt.

The bull had an agreeable demeanor after that.

Luke's trip to New Castle introduced him to city life. Dr. Mitchell had a little office off in the back of the drugstore.

Luke came back home, excited and eager to tell us about his experience.

"It was people walkin' up and down the streets and goin' in and out of stores!" He said. "It really hurt when that doctor pulled that patch off my head. He ain't getting' a hold of me no more."

"I hope I can go sometime, Luke," I said.

The weather finally broke and beautiful spring days awaited us when we got out of bed.

My brothers loved playing outside and I loved to sit in the oversized swing.

Neighbors nearby gave us cherries and we were so excited. Momma had lots to can. Luke and Ben climbed up in the tree and picked the cherries and put them in a two gallon bucket tied to a string.

When it got full, they lowered it. I emptied it and sent the bucket back up.

One of the neighbors gave us a big jar of apple butter. I thought that was the best stuff I could ever slap on a biscuit!

CHAPTER TWENTY THREE

The Weakest Link

Momma, stepping out on the front porch one morning, gave the screen door the liberty to slam behind her. "Where is Patsy?" she asked.

After hearing "I don't know" several times, the urgency could be heard in Momma's voice. "Go look for Patsy. She's gone!" We ran in different directions calling Patsy's name.

Toby, standing on the bridge, yelled "Here she is!" Momma ran toward the rickety bridge tormented by thoughts of Patsy laying in the ice cold water.

"Is she alright?" Momma asked, nearing the bridge.

Patsy laid on her stomach on the bridge looking over into the water. Momma let out a long sigh of relief. She scooped her baby up into her arms and started toward the house. "Water," Patsy said, looking over Momma's shoulder and pointing. Momma knew Patsy's love for the water threatened her life.

One evening Ben noticed an animal not too far from him. With its long tail and black coat with a pretty white stripe on it, he thought it to be one of the prettiest cats he ever saw. Approaching it, he stopped and said "Kitty, Kitty," as he put one knee on the ground and put his hand out. Instead of the creature coming toward him, it turned away from him. Ben soon found out there was something very unusual about this cat as it released it's scent into the air. As he walked in the house, everyone in the room looked toward him.

Ben, looking around, said "I saw the prettiest cat, but it sure did smell bad."

So did Ben.

We were enrolled in school as soon as possible. We received free lunches at the new school. They didn't send us off in a room by ourselves while the other children ate, like they did back on the mountain. I thought about the time I left my sweet potato in a brown bag beside the road on the mountain, because I was too ashamed to take it to school. I no longer had to deal with the shame of not having anything to eat, but we were still made fun of because of the clothes we wore. I think we all hated school and I dropped out before finishing the eighth grade.

Having us for a neighbor was quite an experience for the people living near us. They could hardly believe a family consisting of twelve children under the age of sixteen years had moved into their community.

We hardly ever saw a vehicle go by our house and every time one did drive by, we all ran into the yard to watch it.

Daddy continued his job with the railroad back on the mountain. He stayed with a first cousin, coming home only on the weekends. I missed him.

Luke used the two horses to plow the garden. He had to stand on a block of wood to put the harness on the horses.

The garden at our new house yielded much more than the soil back on the mountain. Kind neighbors brought groceries, and nice clothes without holes in them, to my family.

Daddy and Momma had managed to make a better life for us. Momma knew Jesus was faithful. We even had garden vegetables to share with the neighbors that summer.

I wondered if Jesus would be faithful to me, too. I kept praying to Him.

Luke and Toby went to help one of our kind neighbors one day. The elderly lady fixed them some lunch and brought them a dark colored drink with ice in it. She asked them if they wanted sugar in it. They said "no," thinking the drink was some kind of dirty water. They said it tasted something awful, but they forced it down. Luke later developed a real liking for iced tea once he tasted it with sugar added.

Uncle Collin, lived about thirty miles from our new house. He and Aunt Grace came to visit often. He had two teenage boys and had not been around little girls.

"Come here, Patsy," said Uncle Collin. The toddler ran to his arms. "Give me a kiss," Uncle Collin continued. Patsy wrapped her small arms around his neck, pulling him close, and kissed him on the cheek.

After several visits, Uncle Collin asked Daddy if Patsy could go home with him and his wife. Momma agreed, knowing Patsy's attraction to the creek was increasing.

Uncle Collin's love for Patsy, barely two years old at the time, led to her moving in with him and his wife. The three came back often to visit.

The family chain had been broken by the weakest link.

The dawning of the days ahead brought many changes to our family.

Patsy's absence offered relief to Momma knowing her baby would be away from the danger of the creek and in a home where she was well provided for.

CHAPTER TWENTY FOUR

Maggie Comes Home

Shortly after Patsy moved in with Uncle Collin and his wife, Maggie finished out her school year and came home. She had to enroll in the new school, too.

Momma held Maggie back one year when she first attended school, so Ben could walk off the mountain with her. Momma didn't want a small child walking alone. As a result, Maggie seemed to learn a little faster than the rest of us.

Maggie loved the place, too. I was so glad to see Maggie. I really missed her. It seemed like the time went by fast, though. We were all so happy to have a better life.

Maggie said she missed Patsy. I missed her, too.

When Uncle Collin came to visit Momma and Daddy, he'd sometimes bring his wife's nephew, Robert Nichols with him. Bobby, as we called him, began to date Maggie. Bobby had been married before and his first wife died giving birth to his only child, a son.

"Mr. Compton, I'd like to talk to you", said Bobby, approaching Daddy one evening. I was standing near the window listening to the two of them talking out on the front porch. I kept out of sight, very carefully peering out the window to see what was going on. Maggie stood by Bobby's side holding his hand.

The old chain attached to the wooden swing made a creaking noise as it resisted Daddy forcing it to move back and forth.

"What's on your mind, Bobby?" Daddy responded.

"Well, Mr. Compton, I, I want to marry Maggie." Bobby stammered.

"How do you feel about this, Maggie?" Daddy asked, looking directly into the eyes of his oldest daughter.

Maggie's response came slow, "I want to marry him too, Daddy."

I knew Maggie didn't really want to marry him, but he offered a way out of a life caring for all them young'uns'. Maggie and I had laid in bed whispering at night and I knew they were planning to marry.

"If that's what you want, then you got my blessins'". Daddy's words yielded a son-n-law shortly thereafter.

I missed Maggie something awful. I was left to help feed all those brothers. It sure was a house full. However, the diapers had ceased and it made life a little less demanding. I was so thankful to be off that mountain!

The days turned into weeks and I knew it would soon be time to go back to school. However, I was in for a big surprise before going back to school!

I got to go to Lancaster, Pennsylvania for a week and visit Spencer, who was married by this time. He came and got me in his nice car. I was so excited to go to another state. I thanked Jesus for making the way. I didn't get carsick then, either,

Lancaster was the prettiest place I'd ever seen. There was so much to see. I got to ride in a buggy pulled by a horse. I could eat all the hot dogs I wanted. I really didn't want to go back home, but I knew Momma needed me.

While I was away in Pennsylvania a young man who lived nearby came to visit my family. He heard that a family moved into the community and among them were two good looking girls, talking about Maggie and me, of course. Momma told me all about him. She said he drove a black car, dressed real nice and wore a watch. I didn't think I'd ever get to see him, even though he seemed like an answer to my prayers.

One day, unexpectantly, I received a note from him in the mailbox. The note instructed me to write him if I wanted to go to the movie with him on Saturday. I responded "yes," but knew I'd have to get Momma and Daddy's permission. I prayed and prayed to Jesus that I'd be able to go. Even though I had never seen the man before, going to a movie sounded better than cooking and washing dishes.

Momma and Daddy agreed as long as we took somebody with us. I could hardly wait until Saturday. I knew Jesus was making plans for my life!

On Saturday a big black car came up our driveway. I went out to meet the stranger. I was getting' a little nervous about going with him. Besides, I had got milk on my clothes while milking the cow.

"Hello," I spoke first. "My name is Christine, Easter Christine Compton. I was born on Easter Sunday and some people call me "Bunny.""

"I'm glad to meet you, Christine. My name is Harold Saunders," continuing the conversation, he said, "I'm so glad you can go with me."

"Well, I don't know if I can or not, cause I got milk on me this morning milkin the cow. These are the best clothes I got." I told him, while glancing down at the ground, too ashamed to look at him.

"It don't matter 'bout that. It ain't nothin' wrong with hard work," he said.

I could tell right off he was a kind, hard working person.

He got out of his big black car and we went to the house and I introduced him to my family. He only had two brothers and one sister.

"I don't know if I can remember all these names or not, Mr. Compton," he laughingly told Daddy.

"Oh, you'll get used to 'em," I assured him.

Momma looked Harold straight in the eye and said, "You can take her, but you gotta take Toby with you."

None of us had ever seen a movie before. Harold bought us popcorn and a hotdog. I enjoyed that more than watching the movie! I had the best time and couldn't wait to go again.

Momma said I could go with him again as long as I took one of the others along. One time Momma went with us and fell asleep. While she was snoring, Harold kissed me.

And so began a courtship with Harold Saunders. He bought me my first hamburger at a drive-in movie.

CHAPTER TWENTY FIVE

The Next Move

I overheard Momma and Daddy talking, about moving to Rocky Mount, Virginia and I thought they didn't want me to marry Harold. Me and Toby played "hookie" from school on Monday and we went to Harold's house instead of getting on the bus. He wasn't home at the time but he still lived at home with his parents and they were real nice. We spent the day there and his momma fed us. I was glad to see Harold when he came home for his lunch.

"Harold we got to do somethin' fast, 'cause my family's movin' to Rocky Mount in one week!" I told him when we were alone.

"Where is that at?" asked Harold.

"I saw it on the map at school, but I ain't real sure. Anyway, come to my house early Saturday mornin'," I instructed him.

Toby and I left in time to get home, so Momma would think we'd been in school all day.

Later that evening Daddy asked me "Christine, do you want children?"

"Of course I want children, Daddy!" I answered him.

Daddy then told me something about Harold I didn't know "If you marry Harold you'll never have children, 'cause both of his brothers had two babies that died."

I gasped, but was not about to be discouraged by what happened to his brothers. "Daddy, I want four children and if God wants me to have 'em, He'll give 'em to me. If not, then that's all right, too."

Daddy walked out of the room holding a leather belt in his hand. I thought I was going get a good whoopin', but Daddy was kind. He knew I had done nothing wrong and he just wanted me to have a good life.

Harold arrived at the house on Saturday just before we left for Rocky Mount.

He found out exactly where we were moving to and had Daddy's blessings on visiting us.

Harold helped us move. After we arrived in Rocky Mount, Harold continued his visits. On one occasion, he stayed one week, helping Daddy clear farmland. He didn't want anything in return. He only wanted to be near me. Daddy had agreed to clear the land in exchange for rent.

Harold and I wanted to get married. Momma didn't much like it. With Maggie gone, Momma needed me to help take care of my younger siblings, but I wanted my own family.

Harold decided to tell Daddy that I was pregnant. I agreed and Daddy insisted we get married right away and took us for our blood test the same day. I hated to see Momma crying and so upset, but I wanted a better life.

Harold took his six hundred pound hog, Old Susie, to the market so we'd have money to start our life together. He got ninety dollars in exchange for the hog.

Daddy witnessed the wedding. I stood beside Harold Saunders in a blue dress he bought for me. After the wedding I gathered up my few belongings and carried them across my arm. I left just days after my fifteenth birthday in 1961 and we lived with his parents for a while. Jesus answered the prayer I prayed before we moved off the mountain.

Even though Momma didn't want me to leave, I loved Harold and felt he could give me a good life. Harold wanted a better life, too. He proved to be a hard worker and a good provider. When we had extra, we shared with my family.

One year after I married, Ben joined the army. He left for Germany, where he spent the next three years. He did send money home occasionally to help care for the family.

Patsy, Me, Maggie and then Ben, all left home within three years.

To Momma a day without washing diapers or breast feeding seemed too good to be true. However, Momma was never without something to do, with eight children still at home.

After Patsy had been with Uncle Collin and Aunt Grace for five years, the couple decided to get a divorce. Patsy came back home to live with the family.

Patsy reached her seventh birthday before Ben came home from the Army. He seemed like a stranger to the child as she didn't remember him before he joined the Army. The new family Patsy had then become part of, after five years of living with her uncle, all seemed like strangers to her. She submersed herself in reading books and enjoyed the weekends and summers she spent with Uncle Collin and his second wife.

Luke graduated High School and signed up with the Marine Corp and later served six years in the Reserves. Not doing well in school, Toby decided to enlist with the Army leaving Momma with five boys and two girls living at home.

The family received sufficient help from neighbors and government assistance. Toby and Luke sent money home on a regular basis to help Momma financially.

Daddy, no longer employed with the Railroad, worked as a farmhand on a nearby farm. Momma finally began to have a better life without the day-to-day struggle. Harold and I started a family, as did Maggie and Bobby. Momma became a grandmother and loved her grandchildren as much as she loved us. She did all she could for all her family.

Momma and Daddy's generosity never changed. They always gave to others and thought about them first. I recall a time when a neighbor's boy needed a pair of shoes. Momma thought since her son was blessed enough to own two pair, she should give the boy one pair of them. That's the way she wanted others to treat her, but she was not treated like that back on the mountain. People just gave us things they were going to discard. Momma never forgot what it was like to be without and helped anyone she could. Her own children never went barefoot again.

We were all growing up fast. Daddy and Momma didn't realize just how soon Jacob, Sawyer and Leon would leave home.

(left to right back row) Jacob, Sawyer, Toby, Luke,
Momma & Daddy
(front row) Dean, Leon, Reggie & Libby

CHAPTER TWENTY SIX

The Empty Nest

What happened on November 1, 1955
changed many lives forever. The United States
government formed a Vietnamese Military

Assistance Advisory Group that later ushered in the Vietnam War. The draft began in 1958 before the war actually began in 1959. It would be much later before the United States would get involved in the combat.

Momma fought a spiritual battle on Black Top Mountain to save her family and now reigned as victor. Desiring to keep her sons from the dangers of the coal mines, she sought a better life for them. At the time Momma didn't know that three of her sons would fight in the jungles of Vietnam.

Jacob graduated High School and signed up for the Navy. He later served in the Army Reserves and became Sergeant before his retirement. Sawyer and Leon dropped out of school and enlisted in the Army, having no idea what lay ahead.

Toby, Leon, and Sawyer answered the call to the jungles of Vietnam.

Momma prayed her sons would win their battle in the jungle just as she'd won hers on the mountain. Momma's faith, unapproachable by a shadow of doubt, never wavered. When Momma spoke about her sons in Vietnam she always said "God'll take care of 'em in Vietnam the same as He would if they's here."

The younger children tried to grasp what was happening so far away and often feared the worst.

One afternoon Patsy, Libby and Reggie enjoyed time together in an upstairs room of the two story house they lived in at the time. Patsy decided to go downstairs to get a drink of water. She darted down the steps and reached her hand out to open the door at the bottom of the steps. She froze in her tracks. She heard a sound she never heard before: Momma crying.

Patsy slowly opened the door and looked into the room where Momma stood talking to a man. Patsy noticed he had on a nice suit. She knew instinctively, that whatever he had said had made Momma cry. She heard him mention Leon by name.

With Leon in Vietnam and a strange man talking to Momma and Momma crying, Patsy could only come to one conclusion. She began to cry, too, as she made her way back up the steps.

"Leon is dead," said Patsy to Reggie and Libby, now with tears streaming down her face.

"Are you sure?" asked Libby

"There's a man all dressed up talkin' to Momma and she's cryin'. He's gotta be dead. What else could it be?" Patsy could barely say the words.

"Reggie, we gotta go find out. Come on," said Libby.

The two started down the steps, leaving Patsy behind.

Thinking about her brother, Patsy sobbed, heartbroken at the thought of losing him. She began to tremble. She heard footsteps on the stairs. Glancing up, Patsy saw Libby and Reggie approaching her. Libby hugged Patsy assuring her, "It's alright, Patsy, Leon is alive. Momma was talking to a preacher and he prayed for Leon."

Momma always told us,"You might as well laugh as cry," and her tears were rare.

Patsy never forgot that day when Momma cried.

In later years Leon told us while he was in Vietnam, three missiles fired from the enemy camp and one landed about six feet from him, but didn't go off. I always wondered if that was the same day Momma cried.

Toby, injured and missing for three days in Vietnam put Momma's and Daddy's faith on trial in a way they had never imagined.

Toby went on to receive a Purple Heart, among many other honors. He served his country for twelve years and became a Sargent.

Dean and Reggie were soon on their way to serving their country. Dean chose the Marine Corp and Reggie chose the Navy.

Momma hugged eight sons goodbye as they left, one at a time, to serve their country.

Libby married a man in the Army and they lived in Hawaii for a while. Reggie, in the Navy at the same time and stationed in Hawaii, spent much time with his sister there.

One by one, Momma hugged each of her sons as they returned home once again. God had heard and answered her prayers.

Each of my eight brothers received an honorable discharge from whatever branch of service they chose.

Things were going good for Momma. She and Daddy moved into their first home in Christiansburg, Virginia, purchased with Black Lung benefits Daddy received. After only a few months of enjoying their own home, Daddy had a stroke. As a result his left arm was permanently paralyzed and he dragged his left leg behind him while walking with the assistance of a cane.

Patsy married Harold's cousin at the age of fifteen and moved to Craig County, just weeks after Daddy had the stroke. Jacob and Sawyer married two sisters the same year.

The stroke had a very negative effect on Daddy. No longer the humble man Momma married, he became angry at times and difficult to please. He moved back on the mountain for a few months, staying with friends, but eventually moved back in with Momma.

They sold the house in Christiansburg and purchased one close to Patsy. Libby and Reggie moved to Craig County within the next year.

Daddy became too difficult for Momma to care for. He stayed with Maggie a while. He also spent time with Jacob and his wife. Later, he was moved to a nursing home. Six years after the stroke, Daddy went to be with his Lord on February 1st, 1981. Three days later a small graveyard in Craig County held his remains.

Momma celebrated her fifty-eighth birthday four months later. I recall her saying that she saw every good thing Daddy had ever done in his lifetime.

And the house felt empty.

CHAPTER TWENTY SEVEN

The Full Trees

We were all glad to have Momma living in Craig County, especially since she never learned to drive. We were able to take her places and she lived within walking' distance of a grocery store.

Momma's sense of humor can never be forgotten.

Reggie, while visiting Momma, walked to the store above her house. He'd gone to get some groceries while Momma and Patsy were cleaning house. Thirty minutes passed and the ladies heard someone at the storm door. The main house door stood open.

Momma, assuming it to be Reggie with an arm full of groceries, yelled "Tear the door down!" They were answered with silence so they went to the door and found a complete stranger there. I don't recall why he was there, but I don't think he ever came back.

Another time Reggie had one of his friends at Momma's. After conversing for a while, the subject changed to burglary and Reggie said, "Well, you can't shoot anybody unless they're actually inside your house."

Momma spoke very seriously "Why kill 'em on the outside and drag 'em inside!" I don't think she ever saw Reggie's friend again, either.

Before Daddy died, Tom Mitchell, helping Momma and Daddy move from Montgomery County to Craig County, stepped inside the house and asked Momma what he could do to help. Mom picked up one of her prettiest potted plants and handed it to him, saying "Here, you can take this."

Later that evening, after arriving at the other house, Momma asked "Patton, do you know where any of my plants are? I'm missing one. I gave it to Tom to carry out."

Daddy said "Well, Clarie, I was gonna get that outta his truck and he said you told him to take it." Momma was real careful how she worded things after that.

In spite of Daddy being gone and Momma being alone, she was always joyful, living life to the fullest. Doom and gloom found no entrance way into her soul and she never thought about taking anxiety or depression medicine.

Momma went ginseng hunting above my house often and came back one time with a little more than ginseng; she killed a big rattlesnake! But that rattlesnake seemed small in comparison to what she overcame in her life.

Momma enjoyed the companionship of her children. The children that had been such a burden to her all those years had now become a blessing. Momma loved to go out to eat and shop. Patsy, Libby or I took her on a regular basis.

God promised not to leave her. He hadn't left her on the mountain and now Momma saw Him every day through her offspring. Her needs were always met, as we all contributed in some way to make her life better. Whether it meant a haircut, cutting her toenails, grocery shopping, mowing the grass or balancing her checkbook, we took care of Momma.

Momma sold the house and bought a new single wide manufactured home. She moved near Patsy and helped care for her two children. Jacob built an addition onto the home, so Momma could have a cook stove and a back porch complete with a swing. It was furnished with a brand new washer and dryer, but she never used the dryer. She still insisted on hanging her clothes outside on a clothesline to dry.

Momma inspired everyone she met. She always saw the glass half full, never half empty.

An empty nest resulted in a full tree.

CHAPTER TWENTY EIGHT

A Virtuous Woman

Clara Bell Arnold Compton graced this world with her presence on June 21, 1923 and grew up in the mountains of West Virginia. She traveled far from the place of her upbringing, but never forgot her humble beginnings. Two of her twelve children also came into the world on June 21st; Jacob and Patsy.

Love for the mountains found a permanent abode with Momma. Her love for ginseng hunting and cracking black walnuts became evident. She received as much as one thousand, two hundred dollars at one time for her ginseng. The black walnuts often brought twelve dollars a pound. Momma found simple ways to supplement her small income. She insisted on having a cook stove in her kitchen.

Gathering edible plants, even though she could buy her necessities, took her into familiar territory she loved. I remember back on the mountain when I was ten years old. Momma told me to watch the babies and she picked up the galvanized bucket used when milking a cow. An hour later she'd bring it back full of edible plants. She loved the smell of them cooking. She watched God put those plants on the mountain side right where she needed them. She knew just where to look for them. Her deep-rooted love for the mountains had a special God-given wisdom as its comrade. She taught us to live off the land and not depend on others.

Momma still had a rain barrel after moving from the mountain and the water was used to fill a wringer washer. Years after her children left home, Momma became acquainted with an automatic washing machine. We'd never dreamed of such a thing back on Black Top Mountain.

Momma sometimes went to stay in a house Dean and his wife, Hannah, owned. Hannah lost her mother at a young age and loved Momma dearly. The house sat next door to theirs and they enjoyed Momma's visits.

Momma also enjoyed the company of male friends, though never romantically.

At Christmas the smell of fresh baked apple cakes filled the air. Bowls of food hid the table top. Big homemade biscuits, like the ones back on the mountain, found a place on every plate. Momma's humbleness and joy filled the room as we all thanked God for the bountiful meal on her table. With glass plates piled high, we enjoyed a meal fit for a king. However, her love and encouragement remained our greatest blessing; always there in our life, even during the time when a table served little purpose.

At Christmas time, Momma sat in her rocking chair and opened gifts from us: a robe, a red hat, a pair of shoes, or a bedspread. Momma done her best to provide for us and now we could provide for her. Ben and Sawyer slipped money in her hand when nobody was looking. Momma put it in her pocket and waited until everyone left to look at it.

Momma told each of us "It's not what you've done in your life that matters, it's what you do with the rest of it that counts." She knew each new day was a new beginning and took advantage of it.

Her children afforded her opportunities she could never have imagined while on Black Top Mountain.

And she gratefully accepted those opportunities.

CHAPTER TWENTY NINE

Far And Wide

Toby married and moved to Pheonix, Arizona. That paved the way for Momma to take her first plane ride. Later, she went to Los Angeles three times to visit Reggie. She loved traveling and meeting people. This is the story Patsy told about their travels:

"Momma, can you believe it?" Patsy asked.

"Well, you know the Lord can do anything," replied Momma.

Patsy knew Momma had soared over many spiritual mountaintops in her lifetime. God's reward for her faithfulness took her to a whole new level. The words of Isaiah came to mind: *"They that wait upon the Lord will renew their strength, they shall mount up with wings as eagles, they shall run and not be weary, they shall walk and not faint." Isaiah 40:31*

The plane sped down the runway and lifted off the ground, pushing Momma and Patsy back in their seats. Gripping the armrest and not wanting to miss anything, they looked out the plane's window in disbelief. The small town they left behind became smaller and smaller as the plane moved upward.

Others on the plane sat back in their seats at ease, making it obvious that Patsy and Momma had not flown before. When the plane no longer ascended, it seemed much more comfortable to the two and they released the armrests.

"Oh, Patsy look here. Ain't they pretty?" Momma asked as she leaned back, making it easier for Patsy to see out the window.

"Oh, wow!" Patsy exclaimed, looking at the white fluffy clouds.

After a short airplane ride to a much larger airport, the two women stepped off the plane. The airport in Charlotte, North Carolina seemed huge compared to the one they just left. Patsy, checked her ticket several times, and read the signs overhead. With Momma following her, Patsy turned right and walked briskly.

Momma sat down on a chair while Patsy proceeded to a counter. With two boarding passes in her hand, Patsy turned from the counter, just in time to hear her mother say "I'm goin' to visit my son in Arizona. This is our first plane ride."

Patsy breathed a sigh of relief when she saw the elderly lady sitting beside Momma. The two ladies continued to talk.

The speaker in the airport announced departures. When the airline informed them they could board the plane, Patsy and Momma picked up their bags and followed the others, not sure what to expect. Once on the plane, Patsy explained to Momma she needed to be careful who she talked to.

"Well, you don't have to trust everbody, but you do have to trust somebody," Momma responded.

Patsy changed the subject, realizing the wisdom of Momma's words.

As the two stepped off the plane in Arizona, Toby and his wife awaited them and quickly approached. After hugging each other, they headed for the baggage terminal to pick up their luggage.

One by one, the duffle bags and suitcases started to come out a chute. They began to go around a carousel. Others standing by grabbed a bag as luggage came toward them. One suitcase came by them with the top open. Toby quickly reached out and pushed it back together as it went by them.

"That one is mine," exclaimed Patsy, pointing to a dark suitcase. "Grab it!"

With her luggage in hand, Patsy watched for Momma's. The suitcase Toby had closed came by them again and was now open again. He reached out and pushed it back together once more.

"I wonder where Mom's luggage is." Patsy looked concerned, watching the strange suitcase, which was open again, getting closer.

"That's it right there!" said Momma pointing to the open luggage.

"Really?" asked Patsy as Toby grabbed it with both hands.

"Yes. That's it!" responded Momma.

Patsy glanced at Toby, knowing he had to wonder how the two got there if they couldn't even identify their own luggage.

"It looked so different open," Patsy said, trying to hide her embarrassment.

Time spent with Toby, being more than pleasant after their first plane ride, encouraged the mother and daughter to fly again.

Toby and his family eventually left Arizona, moving to Colorado. Momma, Dean, Hannah and Momma's sister, Aunt Sarah flew there to visit Toby.

Momma later flew to Los Angeles, California three times to visit Reggie, once going into Mexico with Patsy and Reggie.

Dean called Reggie after Reggie and Patsy had a day planned at Sea World and the San Diego Zoo with Momma. He insisted they take Momma to Mexico so she could say she had visited another country. Patsy rented a car and didn't stop on the U.S. side of the border like she was supposed to and drove right into Mexico. (Back at that time it was fairly easy to cross the border.) So Momma ended up in Mexico, all right. Patsy couldn't read any of the road signs in Mexico, so she could have kissed the American soil when she got back on it. Once back in the U.S., Patsy parked the car and they walked across the border. To them, Tijuana seemed like one of the ten worst vacation spots in the world. They felt the restrooms were so bad they couldn't use them. (I can't imagine how bad they were since the three of them had all been introduced to an outside johnny house.)

Nonetheless, Momma could say she'd been to another country. She must have liked it somewhat since she brought her sons and sons-n-law t-shirts from there. When asked about it, they could tell everybody Momma had been there and brought them back t-shirts. I'm sure it was an adventure none of them forgot.

After visiting Sea World and the San Diego Zoo, Patsy said Momma didn't care for the smelly animals, but she did enjoy Sea World.

On one of her visits, Momma, Reggie and Patsy went to Yosemite National Park. Reggie stood mesmerized by the beautiful waterfalls and didn't realize Momma was not at his side.

Patsy walked up to Reggie and asked, "Where's mom?"

With a puzzled look, Reggie replied, "I don't know. I thought she was with you."

Reggie and Patsy didn't have to look very far to see Momma. Instead of approaching the sixth highest water fall in the world and the highest in the United States, Momma stopped at a nearby stream to gather small rocks to take home. It evidenced Momma's appreciation for the little things in life. She loved the outdoors. She never forgot her upbringing in the mountains of West Virginia.

For the next twenty years Momma enjoyed traveling far and wide, even going to Los Vegas,

Nevada with Ben and his wife. Her eight daughters-in-law loved her like she was their own mother. Ben bought Mom a guitar and she loved playing it. She also loved gospel bluegrass music and never had cable television after Daddy passed away. She preferred to listen to cassette tapes and watch VCR tapes. She loved the color red, especially red hats.

Momma spent time at the beach with us and enjoyed camping trips with Maggie and her daughter. She loved life, but always told us that "somethin' would come along and take you out of this life. If God meant for you to stay here, He'd give you a perfect body."

And she was right.

CHAPTER THIRTY

Separated and United

There we sat in a very familiar restaurant; Me, Patsy, and Momma.

"I'm goin' to the bathroom," said Momma, pushing her chair back away from the table. Patsy and I watched Momma go in the opposite direction of the bathroom.

"Momma!" Patsy said the words as loud as she could without disturbing others around us. "The bathroom is that way," she pointed.

Momma turned and headed in the right direction looking somewhat embarrassed.

We began to question why she was spending so much time in bed, no longer cooking very much and seemed to be very confused about her medicine, among other things. In the months that followed we watched helplessly as Alzheimer's began to take control of her mind. We took turns seeing to her needs and let her live alone in her apartment as long as we could.

After a bout with the flu, Momma's mental health rapidly declined and she was placed in a rehabilitation facility and then went to assisted living for a while. Reggie moved to Virginia from California and spent much time taking care of Momma at home. Eventually, Maggie moved in with them to help care for Momma.

Jacob and his wife opened their home and their hearts to Momma. She lived her last days with them.

For the next four years we did all we could for Momma. She still enjoyed shopping and eating out.

Momma lay bedridden for two weeks before meeting Jesus face to face. One by one, her twelve children took her frail cold hands and held them tight. The same hands that held us close so many times, prepared meals, carried water and wood, hoed a garden, dug ginseng, and cracked walnuts. All those things seemed small compared to the times they folded in prayer. Her steadfast faith would soon become sight.

Just like when Momma left Black Top Mountain, she faced what lay ahead and never looked back. Patsy tearfully sat by Momma's side for hours the day before her passing, thankful for the opportunity to thank Momma for all she'd done for her, including helping her raise two sons.

The evening of November 11, 2007, hospice informed us Momma had only a few hours left. Children and grandchildren waited, talked, laughed and cried as we watched Momma go her last mile. Patsy held one hand and Libby the other. When the shallow breathing stopped, they let go, knowing another hand would lead her the rest of the way. It was just past one a.m. on November 12, 2007 (officially Veteran's Day) when Momma went on to the *real* promised land she sang about so many times.

Ironically, Momma is resting beside her beloved Patton on top of a mountain in Craig County. She will leave that mountain behind one day when the trump of God sounds and the dead in Christ rise. There will be no more tears to fall from her eyes. No more pain or heartache will be present there. She is more than a conqueror through Jesus!

Momma's influence in this world lives on. As a result of that encounter with Daddy on Black Top Mountain, books have been written, songs have been sung, canvases have been painted, sermons have been preached, God's love has been witnessed, and lives have been changed.

Just twenty-three days after saying goodbye to Momma, my son, Stevie, died as the result of an ATV accident. Everything my Mother believed and lived out culminated in that one moment of time when I heard the words, "He's gone."

Momma's example proved to me that through faith in God there is no mountain too high to climb. If she did it, I can do it. She inspired me in so many ways and taught me how to treat others. Her influence shaped my life.

The sound of her sweet voice is still heard in echoes beyond the tall timbers of Black Top Mountain:

"I am bound for the promised land

I am bound for the promised land
Oh, who will come and go with me
I am bound for the promised land."

The End

Clara Bell Compton

Author's note

I am thankful for a Mother who lived a Godly life in spite of horrendous adversity. I also thank each one who contributed to this book and each one who has taken the time to read it. Thank you, Christine, for giving me the honor to write our mother's story. Special thanks to my niece, Tammy Compton McKee, and my cousin, Ruth White, who helped make this possible. And may *"that man Jesus"* get all the glory.

Patsy Greenway

Epilogue

At the time of this writing, all twelve of Clara's children are living. The youngest is fifty six years old.

Reggie got a paralegal degree. Luke served in the Marine Reserves and was also employed by Norfolk Southern railroad for forty years. All three of his children are Marines.

Leon became a licensed electrician and Sawyer became a licensed plumber.

Libby worked as a security guard and has a daughter who is legally blind. Libby became a widow when her husband drowned.

Toby finished his civil service career with the U.S. Postal Service and eventually moved to Virginia. Leon is the only one that lives outside the State of Virginia. Ten of the brothers and sisters live within forty five minutes or less of each other.

Maggie never remarried after losing her husband in a car wreck. She retired from Wal-Mart.

Patsy is now the only one of the siblings still working on a secular job. Much of her time is spent in the mental hospital where she is employed in the environmental department. Her husband has cancer. Uncle Collin just celebrated his eighty-eighth birthday. He and Patsy remain close.

Ben ended a thirty year career driving a truck by retiring and ended a forty year marriage by divorce. He now travels throughout the country setting up pool tables to turn a profit. He also enjoys playing his guitar and singing.

Dean became disabled in his late thirties after a heart attack. He married a single mother with two children and became a father to them. He raised one biological son with his two adopted children.

Christine worked at Virginia Tech for twenty-two years and received the employee of the year award in 1998 along with two thousand dollars. She was among five recipients who received the award the first year it was given. Virginia Tech is the largest college in the State of Virginia and employs over eight thousand people. Receiving this award, no doubt, is a result of the example of her mother's love and concern for others that she chose to follow.

Christine is very giving to this day, not just to family, but to anyone she can help along the way, even strangers.

Clara lost her oldest grandson to cancer and had a five-year-old sister fatally shot in her presence. Her brother was only eighteen when he died on his first day of employment with the coal mines. A rock crushed him shortly after he sat down to eat his lunch. He had been married only six months.

Seven of the twelve siblings have survived at least one heart attack. Four of the twelve went through a divorce. Jacob, Sawyer and Patsy are all still with the spouses they chose in 1973.

There are no felons among Clara's children.

Clara's four daughters collectively gave birth to twelve children; two girls and ten boys.

Clara had twenty-nine grandchildren, numerous great-grandchildren and one great-great-grandchild at the time of her passing. None of her seven granddaughters have a sister. Her courage and faith have allowed generations to be free from the poverty and hardships of Black Top Mountain.

"The gospel echoes throughout all the earth and the sound is heard in all the world." Psalm *19:4* (Net Bible)

38410810R00150

Made in the USA
Lexington, KY
08 January 2015